A Gifted

A Gifted Man

✦

Memoir of an artist

Joseph

iUniverse, Inc.
New York Lincoln Shanghai

A Gifted Man
Memoir of an artist

iUniverse books may be ordered through booksellers or by contacting:

iUniverse
2021 Pine Lake Road, Suite 100
Lincoln, NE 68512
www.iuniverse.com
1-800-Authors (1-800-288-4677)

Because of the dynamic nature of the Internet, any Web addresses or links contained in this book may have changed since publication and may no longer be valid.

The views expressed in this work are solely those of the author and do not necessarily reflect the views of the publisher, and the publisher hereby disclaims any responsibility for them.

ISBN: 978-0-595-45156-2 (pbk)
ISBN: 978-0-595-89465-9 (ebk)

Printed in the United States of America

Contents

List of Illustrations

INTRODUCTION

All too often memoirs written by living artists are little more than thinly disguised advertisements. Consequently, when Joseph asked me to review the following pages I expected something along those lines. Happily, I was greatly mistaken.

Joseph has written an accurate account of the long and often tedious process of becoming a master engraver. His story is not always pretty, but it is honest.

Some will no doubt find parts of this book disturbing and as a result will quickly put it down. That would be a mistake. Those who read the entire work shall be richly rewarded since it reveals the driving forces that compelled Joseph to pursue a most difficult career.

This memoir is an intensely personal account of a dream and two loves. Joseph's dream of becoming an engraver was not easily achieved and it is unlikely that when he commenced on that journey he realized it would become a love. Yet, as is common with those who follow their own path to produce work for the shear joy of its completion, engraving seduced Joseph. It also becomes clear in this account that Joseph would not have achieved success had it not been for his other love, Franca. She supplies the stability, support, and understanding that allowed him to perfect his craft.

To describe the pursuit of any dream in words is a difficult task. One must therefore forgive Joseph for the occasional awkward sentence or unvarnished comment. His story, however, is compelling for no other reason than he achieved his dream. That in itself is a happy ending.

Herbert Houze

ACKNOWLEDGEMENTS

Special thanks to Tamara Weaver who sat through countless hours of listening to my monotonous voice as she transcribed this book into print. To Mr. Bainbridge Coon for his wise advice to cut out half of the original manuscript and add photos, to Herbert G. Houze for his appreciation for the arts of engraving and to Signor Giovanelli and his wonderful school of engraving. I especially wish to thank the Fire Arms Engraving Guild of America for all the inspiration I found while I was a member.

Finally, heartfelt gratitude to my friends and acquaintances, without whose help and advice, this book would never have seen daylight.

Joseph
December 2005

LOVE INLAID WITH GOLD

Preface

Model 1894 rifle, Tiffany inspired

Upon my writing table lies a notebook, the first one of many that I have filled with my thoughts. Its pages are tattered and stained. Its cover decorated with a thumb-sized gnome wearing a tall red dunce's cap; he is half-hidden in a garden of yellow flowers. Within those pages, I have found the source to recall some of the events of this unusual life, and what a life it has been.

It began with my illegitimate birth. My mother placed me in a foster home soon after I was born, where I experienced childhood terror, molestation, buggery, beatings and broken bones. All of which were healed with the benevolence of my Creator. The understanding counsel, honesty and love my dearest wife Franca. And great Aunt Lillian who protected me as a small unwanted infant, cared for me as a child, nourished me, dressed the cuts and bruises, encouraged my mind to grow, prepared our meals, washed my body, clothes, and my wounds, then held me to her heart, when I was taken away.

Adopted at seven, worked hard and mistreated by my stepfather, until I dropped out of school at sixteen, enlisted in the air force at seventeen, to be thrown out at twenty-two. It had something to do with black marketing, gambling, theft, and an inability to follow orders. Married three times, fathered six children, bankrupt twice, failed at suicide.

December ninth I will celebrate my sixty-ninth year on this earth. As I write this, I am on the patio of my studio beach home here in the state of Guerrero, Mexico. I have Franca, beloved wife and companion for the past twenty-five years with me. Here also is Ace our dog, named after my card playing days. Texas Hold 'Em was the game, I was quite good.

I am sipping a small glass of brandy, a habit picked up in France as a teenager and smoking a cigarette. Habits picked up as a child and have given up trying to quit. Close by I can hear the breathing of the warm Pacific Ocean. On my sun-tanned skin, I feel the moist caresses of the landward breezes. I am happy here in the cool, dark shadows of this palm frond roof.

The writing of this book is the fulfilling of many promises. I have found that the process of putting these memories of life on paper, taking the time to think backwards, to recollect all the loves, hates, surprises and pleasures, has been a soothing experience. By opening wide all these old wounds, the poison inside, has nullified and I am contentedly at peace.

"I urge you not to procrastinate, for on the plains of hesitation, bleach the bones of countless millions who waited and while waiting wasted and died." (Anonymous)

Chapter one

"FINDING DAD"

"You know, mother, I was wondering about my biological father." That is as far as I got when mother went ballistic. "Your biological father!" she yelled. "Ernest is your father! He adopted you, can't you be satisfied, and can't you ever leave well enough alone."

"No, mother, I want to know something of my real father, I am thirty-eight years old, and for all those years I've wondered who the man was. What did he think? What did he do? What was he like?"

She put her drink on the coffee table, got up from the sofa, walked to the hall closet and in a few seconds returned with a small black and white snapshot of a man. She threw it onto the table, and began to cry.

"I was only seventeen and it was the first time. You ruined my life, and because of you, I had to leave school. All because of you." she said sadly. She looked at me, sadly shook her head, and wiped the tears away from the corners of her hazel eyes with her fingertips.

"Here" she sighed, "His name is Wallesky, and he lives in Manchester. You have caused me grief since you were born, you are a misery to me now, and I wish I had never had you. Are you ever going to be satisfied?"

All through out life I have had difficulty with criticism and rejection. Blame it on my childhood, head injuries, whatever. If someone said I could not do something, I would try my damndest to prove them wrong. If told I had to do something, I would resist past the point of pain.

Now that this germ of an idea had formed in my mind, I could not let it go. I had to locate my natural father, I needed to see him, had to see him, a driving curiosity cried to be satisfied.

That evening, I got a copy of the Manchester, New Hampshire phone book, looked up Wallesky. To my surprise there were at least twenty of them listed.

Thus began the search for a dad I had never known. I would dial, someone would answer, and I would introduce myself.

"Hello Mr. Wallesky?"

"Yes, who is this?"

"My name is Joseph, and I would like to ask you a question."

"What?"

"Did you ever go out with a girl named Lilly Beckford?"

"Huh?" Usually this ended the conversation with a bang. Sometimes, I would get further into the questions.

"I'm not trying to cause any problems sir, but I'm trying to find my father. A man named Wallesky dated my mother in 1937 and I am the result. Did you know a Lilly Beckford in 1937 or 38?"

There would be a brief silence and then they would hang up. I had worked the way down the list of Wallesky and was starting on the K's. Wallesky, Karl. I dialed the number, a woman answered.

"Hello?"

"Good evening, ma'am. My name is Joseph and I'd like to speak to your husband."

"I don't have a husband"

"I'm sorry. I was calling for Karl Wallesky; must have dialed the wrong number."

"Oh, Karl," she said. "He's here, just a second please. I waited; then heard a muffled voice yell, "Karl, somebody's on the telephone."

Presently, Karl's pleasant voice came over the receiver. "Hello"

I came straight to the point. I had repeated the question so many times that it was down pat, no stumbling, and no mumbling.

"Mr. Wallesky, my name is Joseph, I live in Derry. My mother dated a man with your last name back in 1937 and I'm the result. I don't want to cause you problems or anything, but did you ever know a girl named Lilly Beckford, sir?"

There was a dead silence on the phone. I was trying to think of what else to say next when he said.

"By God, you've got the right fellow."

I explained once again that I wished to cause him no harm, only to satisfy my mind. I offered to meet for lunch or beers.

"No," he replied. "Come on up its ok."

I found him living in a small but comfortable second floor apartment. A blonde woman close to his same age answered my knock on the door.

"You must be Joseph," she said. "Come in."

Karl had just gotten up from his recliner; he was a short, handsome looking man who had aged well. We took a few steps toward each other and then stopped. We looked at each other straight in the eyes. Then, a vision I could never accurately describe began to whirl through my mind. I could see the future standing before me.

I had at last found the missing part of me. Karl was 67 years of age and in conversation, he told me I had seven half brothers and sisters; I turned out to be a lot like my real dad. The woman who had answered the door was Karl's friend, his wife having passed away. He had retired as a supervisor for one of the many shoe-making manufacturers in the area

We talked for a very brief while, perhaps twenty minutes, I told him where I lived, and that I worked repairing guns for a living. Karl's friend offered me a beer, opened one for her self, and gave Karl a fresh bottle then we sat for a while making uncomfortable small talk. They invited me to stay for dinner, feeling ill at ease, and intruding I thanked them, left them my phone number with a promise to get back together again for dinner.

"I'll give you a call," were the last words. I heard dad say.

He never did and I never contacted him again. However, I had finally put a very confusing puzzle piece of life in its place.

I recently had purchased several new machine tools for the gunsmith business. And, as ever, was paying for them on time. My income was sufficient to maintain everything and all was financially well.

My second wife, a Dixie belle named Loretta, who preferred the name Red, was content; there was money for, booze, the new Monte Carlo, dancing and partying until 2 a.m. Then suddenly, my largest client decided insurance costs were prohibitive and discontinued my services,

The loss of their business meant the loss of the Monte Carlo. I gradually fell behind on its payments, until one morning, thirty years ago; I climbed out of bed, and as usual looked out the window.

Where I had parked the brand new Monte Carlo, there was now, nothing but a blank space.

In shock, I said "Holy shit someone has stolen our new car"!

Red rolled over; lazily opened her green eyes, looked at me, sadly shook her head, and said, "Call the cops."

I called the cops and reported the theft; an officer told me to hold the line. While I waited, the thought that mother was right repeatedly kept entering my mind.

Soon a voice said, "Joseph LaVarnois,"

"Yes sir," I answered as my stomach began to knot in pain …

"Your car was picked up this morning by the HFC finance company, I suggest you contact them."

"Shit "I cried as I slammed down the receiver," Oh shit."

Red sat on the edge of the bed while I explained to her where the car went. I could not believe I was going down the rat hole another time. My mother was right, I was worthless, I caused nothing but misery to everyone I loved, I was better off dead than living. I might as well blow my brains out as continue. It just was not worth continuing.

I dressed, went downstairs to the basement, to the workshop where John, my apprentice was already at his workbench polishing guns for re-finishing.

"Hi," he said as I hit the bottom step and walked over to the workbench, I ignored him and did not answer. I was so close to tears that I did not trust my voice. On the bench were several handguns that had been repaired, I picked up a small 38 Colt automatic, loaded it and stuck it in my jeans pocket.

"John, they just repossessed the damned car."

He said nothing; did not try to stop me. I knew he understood. I said walking out the basement door,

"John, don't come after me I need to sort all this God damned crap out."

"Just think it over," was his reply.

With all the weights of the past pressing down on me, I walked around the house, stood in the empty spot of the drive where the Monte Carlo had been. Stopped, turned around and looked up at the bedroom window where Red most likely had gone back to sleep. Said goodbye to her, stuck my hand into my jeans pocket, felt the cold steel of the slender automatic, turned, and crossed the highway and entered Hood's Meadow.

Hood's Meadow was one of the few places nearby that reminded me of my youth and the dairy farm where I spent the first seven years of my unusual childhood ... A footpath led through the tall pines. The fragrance of resin was in the air, a beautiful day ... Nevertheless, I felt no joy. For the forest was to become my tomb.

As I walked through the woods, I felt a presence there with me. Soon the dark sunless shadows of the glade lightened and opened onto the lovely meadow. In the distance, I could see the white spire of the Derry Village church. I found a large stump of an old oak tree and sat down. I sat for the longest while, head bowed, eyes open, not thinking or seeing, and then I began to cry. Long sobs emanated from the pit of my stomach, I wept until there was not a tear left within my soul.

"God, I am a profane, fornicating, lying, sordid man who has no right to ask for anything. Please help me" and more tears began to flow.

It was at this moment a young woodchuck came out of its den close by; the movement of its body caught my eye. I watched it sit up and look carefully around, and then begin to eat the greening leaves of the shrubs.

I suddenly began to talk to the small harmless animal that I had once killed with a bloody ferocity in my youth.

Drawing from memory

"I wish I were you," I said to it. "You do not care a damn about your family. You have no rent to pay or car to lose. You live in peace. You are one of God's creations." Miserably I thought "God."

I wondered. Why was I on this planet? If all life has a purpose, what is mine? What am I doing here with this pistol in hand ready to splatter my brains over the green grass of this meadow?"

It then occurred to me that perhaps why I ended up here so low and lost, was because I would not believe or kneel. I sat there for the longest while, trying to make some sense out of my unhappy life. Everything had come to failure and degradation, I had lost every thing I had loved and worked for, during the fifteen years of my first marriage: wife, home, business, and most importantly the parenthood of children whom I dearly loved.

Now this second marriage was beginning to crumble. What could I do? How was I to obtain the respect of the omnipotent force in the Galaxy? The only good thing about me, as far as I was concerned, was the ability to use my hands. Marcelle, my first wife, always said I had hands made of gold.

The woodchuck suddenly whistled in alarm, arousing me from those sad thoughts. I slowly lowered the hammer of the pistol, as I did so a thought entered my mind. Maybe, just maybe, I am here on this earth to set an example. Perhaps if I devote myself, He will notice me drowning. At that precise second, the Presence intervened.

"I will help you." A voice said.

Then an idea came to me, I would become an engraver.

I would dedicate my work to the Universal spirit, God if you will, a tree if you wish, and when I had succeeded I would write a book to repay this debt.

Gaining the universal-spirit's respect was a huge if not impossible task for the kind of a man I was … Me, a broke, lying, stealing, profane, atheist who was repairing junk guns and Saturday night pistols.

"God is going to notice me. Fat chance of that happening, maybe when hell freezes over," I said aloud.

"Stop lying," the Presence clearly said. "First you must stop lying to others; your brain is so full of lies that it won't function. Start telling the truth."

I had the vision of a customer asking if I had stolen the firing pin I was replacing in his gun and me replying, "Yes, I stole it from the gun dealer who dropped my services."

"Stop stealing, do these two simple things is all I ask" the Presence had spoken again.

I got up from the stump, unloaded the pistol, made my way home. It was then that I started writing in a journal. The first entry reads

God exists and one day I will prove it.

Joseph,
June 14th, 1980

Chapter two

"REDEMPTION IN ART"

The change from teller of lies to teller of the truth is not as hard as it sounds. The truth is that once you have cleared your mind of those petty thought-absorbing lies, you function much better. Just open your mouth and out tumbles the truth. It is that simple. The same practice applies for not stealing. You just do not do it. The excuses: "They don't need it," "They'll never know," "I have to have it" no longer influence you. You do not earn or buy self-respect; it can only come as a gift. "I'll try one more time to be someone," I thought while walking back home.

With a deeper resolve than I had ever had in any endeavor before, started my engraving career.

I had purchased some used engraving tools and had been trying them out from time to time, but now I became serious about it. I contacted Mr. Winston Churchill, the famous engraver who lived in Vermont and asked his advice. He recommended that I find employment with a company that dealt in expensive engraved weapons.

"That would give you a chance to look closely at the engravings and better understand the art," He said.

One of the companies Mr. Churchill recommended was the Paul Jaeger Company in Jenkintown, Pennsylvania. They were responsive to my inquiries for employment; quickly an interview date was established. I had found enough money to buy another car, a 1967 Ambassador station wagon. Its tires were balding and it burned some oil. I got it from a used car and junk dealer down the road.

"No credit? Bad credit, we can help."

The financial transaction consisted of the welder, shotgun, and color T.V. Red and I left John in charge of things and made the trip down to Jenkintown, where I met with Dietrich Appelle.

Mr. Appelle was a tall, almost gaunt, gun maker who had apprenticed in Germany. I had brought along a rifle that I had been working on, a model 1892

Winchester that I was restoring. Mr. Appelle looked it over without comment then questioned me further about my job skills. After the interview finished, Mr. Appelle hired me to start as soon as possible. During the interview at Jaeger Company, I made it clear that I wanted to learn to engrave. Mr. Appelle had his own house engraver, also from Germany. His name was Claus Willig, and his works of arts in steel are an absolute wonderment.

Model 1885 Winchester low wall, engraved in Germanic style.

The Company hired me to work, as a gunsmith, directly under the shops headman, an arrogant little Swiss who once worked for one of the best English gun makers. Name was Alfred; he looked like a doctor with round spectacles and upright posture, instead of a white smock, he wore a dirty canvas apron and his hands and fingernails were black.

Once I got off that stump and began planning a career, life suddenly started to take on new meaning. I became religious, not in a fanatical way but in a subdued quiet manner. I did not go spouting off about my beliefs. I just stopped lying, stealing, and started saying everyday.

"Thank you, Lord, for my life."

While I had sat on that stump, I kept thinking, "Who am I? What am I? Why am I? It suddenly came to me. I was Joseph and I was going to be a great artist because I am loved for not giving up."

I had therefore made up my mind before the job interview that I was going to drop my adopted last name.

When Alfred and I shook hands, he asked in his impeccable British accent "And how shall you be called?"

I thought for a second, then answered "Joseph"

"Joseph it is then." I had become a new man with a new interest and new passions ... I enjoyed working at Jaeger's and even though Alfred and I rubbed each other the wrong way from time to time, he was a good man to work with. Through him I learned stock making, rust and charcoal bluing. He helped me to refine my polishing techniques. All these tasks are part of the trade of an engraver of weapons. While working there I also reacquainted myself with the lathes, milling machines, drill presses, welding equipment, etc.

I was looking through the reference library at Jaeger's when I found the book that was to change my life and its direction forever. It became my bible, teacher, and mentor. Its title is, "L'Arte dell'Incisione" authored by Mario Abbiatico, founder of the famous Italian gun maker's firm, Abbiatico and Salvinelli, located in the town of Gardone, Val Trompia, Italy.

No doubt, that Signor Abbiatico's magnificent effort to show the most beautiful works of engraving produced by the Italian school changed my life and me forever.

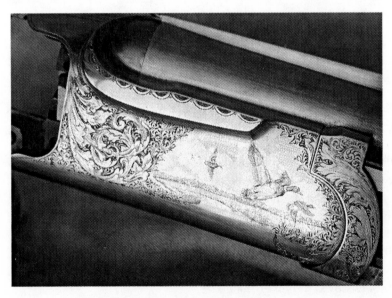

Ruger O/U, inspired by Mario Abbiatico

When I looked through the pages of exquisite engraved weapons, I knew that I must go to Italy. I took it upon myself to write Signor Abbiatico a letter.

Dear Sir,
I am a gunsmith living in the United States. And would like to learn engraving. If I put myself through art school and if, I learn to engrave in this country, would you consider me for an apprenticeship?

I mailed the letter to the address printed inside the book cover. It was a few weeks later that I received a response from Signor Abbiatico:

Dear Joseph,
Now, all engraving positions are full. However, who knows what lies in the future. We are a growing company. Perhaps in the future we could use another employee.

Respectfully yours,
Signor Mario Abbiatico

This short polite letter was contact with another world.

Shortly after our arrival in Jenkintown, I had found a lawyer, Mr. Eric Gold, who listened to my reasons and said he, would do the necessary legal work required to change my name. For three hundred dollars, I could become legally Joseph. I had to make a court appearance and answer some questions asked by the judge, namely "why?" In court, I explained my childhood and the confusion I had over my identity.

"Sir, I wish to have my last name dropped, because I detest the man that gave it to me, and I want to be free of it."

"And what reason do you have for hating this man?" the judge asked.

I looked at him trying to control my emotions; it was very difficult to do, I knew that I would soon start crying.

Mr. Gold answered for me. "Due to this man's extremely difficult childhood, he has a lack of personal identity and wishes to be free of his past and its memories, Your Honor"

"Before I can make a decision you will have to explain your feelings more clearly" the judge said.

Mr. Gold said to me "Calm down, I will handle this for you"

"Your Honor in his infancy, Joseph was placed in a foster farm by his mother, he was of illegitimate birth, and stayed at this farm for seven abusive years. In this time, he recalls seeing his mother once. He was taken away to live with her and the man she had married, a Mr. Ernest LaVarnois, who adopted Joseph at the age of eight and was physically abusive to him. This is the reason he wishes to remove his last name" Mr. Gold replied.

"And what did this man do to abuse your client, Mr. Gold?"

"He whipped him, worked him, and then at the age of thirteen made him shoot his dog, Your Honor."

"Are there any legal consequences, such as property ownership?" the judge asked

"No Sir." Mr. Gold replied.

He granted my request.

With the pressures of self-employment lifted, I started to recover some enthusiasm for living. Red also was happy that I finally had a real job.

There was money again for clothes, to party and dance the night away. One of the things I had decided to do, as "Joseph" was to cut down on the amount of alcohol I was drinking. I knew that as an engraver I would need steady hands. In addition, the hangovers were unpleasant and coming more frequently than I liked. Joseph changed ways. While Red remained true to form, pretty much the party girl.

Another crack appeared in this marriage when I entered Temple University as a night student. I still remember the excitement I felt as I walked through the campus looking for the administration's offices, once in the registrar's office I asked about art classes. I had no idea what I was doing, but knew that a great engraver had to be able to draw and draw well. I explained to the young woman in the office that I wanted to become an engraver and needed to take art classes in order to do so.

I do not think my stubby fingers and steel blackened nails at all impressed her, she politely explained that school was in its last semester, and there were no more classes.

I asked again, "Are you sure there are no classes available?"

A thought suddenly came dancing through my mind, "Wink at her." I looked the woman straight in her brown eyes and winked.

She suddenly smiled then said, "Well, there's the advanced drawing class. It's a very advanced class and I don't know how you'll fit in."

The class had no educational requirements, and it ran five nights a week from seven to nine. The cost was $500, which I could just manage to pay.

School started at Tyler University on January 15, 1981, which was only two weeks away. In six short months, I had gone from a man with a gun in hand, to a man walking on The Creator's plan. I stood a bit prouder and I felt a bit better. I could hold at bay the bitter grief over the loss of custody of my children only by the fact that I knew one day I would return to them, bring to them help and love, be father to them once again.

This thought was constantly with me. I had to recover; somehow, I had to get off the freight train to hell that the divorce judge in Oregon City had placed me on in 1976. It just seemed as if the more I tried to slow that train down, the faster it went, dragging me with it, tearing me to pieces.

Enrollment at Tyler was not at all to Red's liking. She had made the adjustment of being married to a man with one name. She had barely accepted the fact that the old car I had traded for in New Hampshire had finally expelled its last exhaust fumes on a very cold night in Hatboro, Pennsylvania …

The apartment we had rented was ideal for me. It was located on the bus and rail lines, not having a car was hardly an inconvenience. For Red, it was another story. She needed transportation to her new job as a bank teller.

I talked Dietrich into helping finance another set of wheels. He had a red Pinto station wagon that had decent tires and a four-cylinder engine that could hardly get up a hill by itself without a struggle. However, four wheels beats two heels, I bought it from him on credit.

Finally, the day came to start drawing classes. I went to the first class carrying a pad of newsprint sketch paper and some charcoal sticks. I was one of about 30 students, the oldest one taking the class.

It was a drawing from life class, meaning that nude models would pose for the students. Red, did not like it, but went along with it all.

The first model was a well-built and well-endowed black man in his twenties. The teacher directed us to do 10-minute sketches of the model that stood naked on a movable wooden pedestal. We all sat with our drawing tables in a circle around the pedestal. Each student had a different view of the model. Quick sketches were made of the model, and every ten minutes the pedestal rotated a quarter of a turn. I started with a posterior view and ended up with a frontal pose. Halfway through the drawing session the model had developed a full erection. I ignored his ignorance and drew as best I could. I suspected the teacher used the man as a model to get rid of those not too serious art students.

That night I showed Red the sketches. She thought it was funny. However, I did not. The class progressed I was given homework, draw a broccoli, hallways, trees, people, hands, any thing that caught my interest My sketchbook became a constant companion. I started reading, and the more I read, the more I wanted to read. It was through drawing and studying that I was at last able to find a place without torment, where my mind was occupied by a peaceful presence.

While drawing, I felt as if a force was directing my hand. It was during those drawing classes I found myself. I knew what I was good for; I thanked The Universal Spirit every day for such a beautiful gift. Soon, evening classes were not enough. I enrolled in a second art class that took place every Thursday afternoon at the Abington Art Center, the difference being that this model was a beautiful young woman.

The drawing class on Thursday afternoon was a bit of an irritant to Alfred, he started calling me Picasso.

"Oh La, 'ere he is, Picasso his bloody self", He would say as I returned from class to the gunsmith shop. He would always ask to see my drawings.

During one session, I had drawn the model on blue paper with charcoal. When I showed it to Alfred, he commented, "Like bloody Picasso, he's now in the blue period."

Three very important things happened while I was going to art school. The first happened at Tyler.

At the end of the term, students had to post their drawings on the classroom wall, for the teacher to review. I do not recall the man's name, but I am sure he still remembers Joseph. I was the pale man with the haunted eyes, the sad quiet demeanor, the desire to draw, and only one name. One by one, the students passed into his office to have their work critiqued. Came my turn, I entered the cluttered room. The teacher was around 25 years old with a sprout of a beard, John Lennon glasses, long slender fingers, and soft hands.

I was envious of those hands with their soft palms, delicate fingers, and clean nails. What he said there in that office gave me hope to continue.

He said, "Sometimes the teacher can learn from the student. You are an inspiration to me. I am glad to have known you."

We shook hands and I departed from Temple University a man who was sure of his success.

The second incident took place at the Red Barn Apartments. The Red Barn was located in downtown Hatborough. It had actually been a dairy barn, complete with milk cows and equipment. The property owner had converted the barn into two levels, the lower level for businesses and professional offices, the upper contained twelve apartments. All the tenants were our age or younger, single or couples without children. Some nights we would get together outside for burgers, beer and share a joint or two.

The back stairwell led down to an outside grill, it was a simple stairway with walls painted with white primer. It provided me with a large, irresistible, drawing surface. Each evening I would take a charcoal stick and draw on those walls, I drew a nude with her pubic hair at eye level, a five-foot tall sketch. Soon the sketch became a meeting place for the other renters, they would sit on the stairs and watch me draw, drinking beer, and giving anatomical advice on the drawing of Eve.

One evening, shortly after I had finished drawing, we were having burgers and beer outside, the weather was cold, but nobody minded. We were all having a good time. One of the partiers not from the Red Barn, lived somewhere nearby. This man, whom I had never met before needed to urinate. I directed him up to our apartment, when he returned he asked me about the drawing on the stairwell. "Did I want to sell it?" He asked.

I told him that to sell it was impossible, as it would require tearing the whole wall out.

"Would you make a copy? I will pay you to do so, let's say $500 for it, here's half an advance."

That night Red and I celebrated, but later on when she had fallen asleep. I went back to the hallway, sat on the stairs in front of the drawing and cried.

The third incident was at Abington Art Center. I had just finished a three quarter frontal pose drawn with blue chalk of a very beautiful model. I stepped back to look at it, pulling out of the trance-like mood that I am in when drawing, stood in front of the easel and looked at what I had drawn.

It struck me as so beautiful that I felt tears gush to my eyes, quickly I left the classroom and went outside to the empty hallway to let go another stream of tears.

The lawyer who had helped with my name change was a great person, we related. He liked art and had changed his last name from Goldstein to Gold; we became good acquaintances after the completion of my legal business. I stopped by his office one afternoon to show him some sketches.

"Hey Joseph" he smiled and got up from his chair, "I was just thinking about you, How's your new drawing class going?"

"I think it is just great Mr. Gold, I thought you might like to see some new sketches."

I opened the portfolio and showed him several; he had a great admiration for the blue nude, so I gave it to him. I enjoyed giving sketches away.

Now, being sure that I could draw, I started on the second part of my pilgrimage. Needing to find some one who could teach engraving, I borrowed books from Jaegers reference library and looked up the listing of firearms engravers. My good friend Jimmy Tucker mentioned Ken Hurst who was located in nearby Virginia. I contacted him by phone, introduced myself to him, and said I was hoping to learn engraving. My skills as a gunsmith and the fact that I worked at Jaegers impressed him enough to invite me down for a job interview.

Chapter three

"THE RED PINTO"

I have no idea where that letter I received from Signor Abbiatico is or if it still exists, but the return address on it was the ticket to new worlds and new lives. The front of that envelope revealed where that destination was. I had a name, a city, and a country. I needed no more than that. I had completed drawing. I then started working on task number two: Learning to engrave in this country. The metamorphosis had begun.

The following week, Red and I set off for Lynchburg in the Pinto wagon. Life was starting to have some resemblance to normality. Our bills were paid and we were able to save a bit each week, for a trip to Italy. Red and I were having a reasonably good relationship. We never swore at each other, nor were we jealous. Living with Red was a thousand times better than living with Marcelle my first wife, she who tried to stab me with a very big butcher knife that quickly severed our marriage. We had met not long after my divorce. Red liked to party and I was happy to go along. During the time we were together, I always found employment at one job or another and made reasonably good wages. Red was a well-endowed strawberry blond with a fine figure, which she showed off to its maximum effect. We were a handsome couple and were popular at every dance Club or bar we went.

We drove happily into the heart of Baptist country. The home of Jerry Farwell, Virginia hams, mint juleps and the Ken Hearst Engraving Company. Mr. Hearst formerly worked for the Colt Fire Arms Company and received us warmly, he showed us around his shop located on the tenth floor of a gray stone building. There were a dozen engravers and apprentices working there. All of the engravers were about half my age and all were very talented people. Mr. Hearst showed me some of the finished pieces of engraving

I began having some doubts about my ability to engrave. It looked complicated and precise. I stood and watched the engravers working there, listening to the tap, tap, of the small hammers driving sharpened chisels through polished steel. Each engraver was swaying to the synchronized movements of hands, wrists, hips, shoulders and feet, as if dancing to the rhythm of their hammer strokes. All were intently peering through their magnivisors at the delicate lines they were cutting in steel

Mr. Hurst explained the learning process would take about three months, and I would receive no pay until good enough to begin engraving professionally. All that I could gather from Mr. Hurst's appearance and possessions, indicated engraving was indeed a very lucrative trade. Red was also impressed with the money Mr. Hurst seemed to be making. After treating us to dinner at a very nice restaurant, I agreed to start to work after giving notice to Alfred and Dietrich Apelle at Jaegers. It was with great excitement that we drove back to Pennsylvania in the red Pinto, me happy to continue, Red happy to find people with accents she felt comfortable with, while listening to Alabama on the radio.

The following Monday I went to see Mr. Appelle in his office.

"Mr. Appelle, I'm leaving Jaeger's to learn to engrave," I announced.

Dietrich was not at all happy with this and replied,

"You cannot be an engraver; it takes years to learn to engrave. You are a good gunsmith. You should remain a gunsmith. You are too old."

I continued to insist and give my notice. Alfred was not pleased either. I reminded him that I had said all along that I was going to become an engraver.

May, 29th, 1981 (From my notebook) Lynchburg, Virginia

Started to work for Mr. Hurst, three days of cutting metal plates, the same cuts over and over, and over, it looks like I will be doing the same thing for another week. I sure hope it doesn't take much longer as there is no pay until I am actually good enough to engrave a firearm, have very few dollars left and the car is almost out of gas. I am not worried though, for God always provides. We have a nice place out in the country and a cute puppy named Tilly. P.S. It is the first time we have moved without selling all to do it.

June 7th, 1981

Taken a long time just to get a few hundred dollars to work with, but I know with self-control I should be able to keep reinvesting it and have enough to go to Italy in two more years. Please Master; grant us good health, and me the stamina to catch my dreams.

Your creation, Joseph

Sometimes what appears to be a ruinous misfortune turns out to be a blessing in disguise. Red was a good friend and lover. She came along when my life was shattered and I was extremely depressed. She was a vivacious, fun-loving party girl and she was ten years younger than I was. In Lynchburg, we began to have serious problems living together.

I had developed a new set of priorities; I no longer drank to get drunk, she had not. I was working and learning engraving, but the amount of money I was making was very little. I was spending less time with her and devoting more time to drawing. I could sense the change in her; she got moodier as the weeks went by.

One Saturday night after supper, I suggested we go out dancing. There was a club on the outskirts of Lynchburg where the beer was cold and the band was good. It was a rough and tumble roadhouse with a red tin roof, called the 501 Club. It is probably still there.

The owner of the 501 Club was a woman who had seen all of humanity at its worst. Drunkenness, fistfights, knife fights, gunfights, fornication, you name it, Grandmotherly Bea had seen it all. Bea was the woman who sat in front of the swinging doors to the saw dusted, wood dance floor. If you wanted on the dance floor, you had to pay the $3 fee with no exceptions. That night Red put on her sexy new green pantsuit and high-heeled dancing boots, I dressed in jeans and a white shirt and brought along a sketchpad and drawing pen. When we arrived, I drove the Pinto into the nearly full parking lot, found a space near the back, parked, then walked around and opened the door for Red. Together, hand around waist; we made our way into the bar of the 501 Club.

Red and I had been to this club several times before and we were on first name terms with Bea. I knew that Bea would never let us into the dance floor without collecting the cover charge. All the money I had was a ten-dollar bill and a few crumpled ones. I gave them to Red.

"If we both go in to dance, there won't be enough for two beers. You take it, go in, and have a good time. Meanwhile I'll try to make a few dollars doing portrait sketches. When I get some money, I'll join you."

She smiled, I kissed her and watched her disappear through the swinging doors that Bea stood guard over.

It turned out there wasn't a redneck in the place interested in having their likeness put down onto paper, so I sat at the bar, did quick sketches of the pool players and listened to the music of the band. Only one woman was interested in a portrait but she had no money, I settled the price of the sketch at one Coke and a bag of peanuts.

I began roughing out the shape of the woman's head and the volume of her hair, noting the details of her face. It was then that I noticed she had a badly cleft lip. As I sketched it, I minimized the deformity. Once the drawing was completed and before I gave it to her, I checked it over once again. It was only then that I noticed that one of her eyes was way out of alignment. Then I looked at her face again. This time I saw her as a whole object rather than form and shadow. It was not until that moment that I saw she had a distorted head. She was very happy with the sketch and asked me to sign it, which I did. She took the drawing looked intently at it, cooed, then said, "You're just the sweetest fella I ever did meet." Shortly after that, the band took its break. Red appeared through the swinging doors, followed by a tall well-dressed but slightly drunk man who was dressed like the rhinestone cowboy. I got down from the barstool and greeted them. Red introduced me.

"This is my husband Joseph. Joseph, this is Mac. Mac is from Alabama." We shook hands and said hello, then Red said, "Mac has got a new van, its outside. Want to see it?"

"Sure," I replied. We went out to look at Mac's new van. After spending a few minutes admiring the plush interior and pretty much the fact that it was a bedroom on wheels, I agreed with Red that it was indeed a super deluxe van, it even had a bar.

We left the parking lot and walked back into the 501club where the band was getting ready for its next set. Red wanted to know if I had made any money. I explained, no one had any money, and if they did, they were not spending it on portrait sketches. I gave her the little change I had left, encouraged her to go dance and have a good time, kissed her, and walked her to the swinging doors of the dancehall.

Time passed quickly while sitting on that barstool. I was halfway through a sketch of the back bar with its glass, bottles, mirrors, reflections and lights, when the music ended and the partygoers started filing out of the swinging doors. I put away the sketchbook and pen and sat waiting for Red to show up.

Soon the crowd began to dwindle and alas, there was no one left.

"What the hell?" I thought. "I better see what's going on. Where is Red? Probably she is in the lady's room. Maybe she had too much to drink."

I walked over to the now-open doors. A very empty dance floor greeted me. The only people around were the band members and a big guy with a broom pushing a mountain of bottles, cans, and assorted trash towards a garbage can. I walked over to the woman's room, knocked on the door, and then peeked inside.

"Red, are you in here" No answer. "Hey, Red, are you OK?" no one there.

I was so sure she was in there that I entered and started looking in the stalls to see if she had passed out or was sick. Empty. Confused, I went back out on the dance floor. The band players had packed up and headed for the back door.

"Hey guys, you see a good looking redhead wearing a green pants suit?"

"Sure man, she left out the back door about a half an hour ago with some dude," someone from the band answered. I was blindsided. I had not seen it coming. I had no idea. Dumbstruck, I charged out the back door looking for Mac's van. The only vehicle sitting in the darkened parking lot was the red Pinto and the band's pick up. Mac's new van was nowhere in sight.

"He's gotten her drunk and kidnapped her," I thought as I ran around to the other side of the club expecting to find Mac, his van and kidnapped wife. It was empty and very deserted, abandoned, a black nothing, only the Pinto with its balding tires to meet my dejected eyes.

"Please don't let this happen. I've been trying," I thought while walking back to the reliable Pinto.

I drove downtown, checking the all-night restaurants, the local motels, and any all-night establishment I could think of … all empty, totally void, no signs of Red or Mac's rocking and rolling van.

Around 4 a.m., I called the Lynchburg police department and reported Red missing. The person I talked too listened to this tale of woe and then asked me for the details, when I mentioned the 501 club, he interrupted me.

"I see," said the voice on the line sympathetically. "I'm sorry but we can't help you now."

"What do you mean you can't help me now? I groaned in desperation, "some guy from Alabama's got my wife?"

Finally, he explained, that, to file a missing person report, twenty-four hours had to pass. Despondent I drove back to our two months-behind in rent trailer house, where our four-month-old Dobby named Tilly greeted me. She was whining and wiggling at my feet as I unlocked the kitchen door.

"Come here Tilly," I muttered. Picked her up and holding her to my chest, carried her onto the sofa where I crashed, a deceived, confused, 41-year-old man.

Somehow, I made it to bed, lay my distraught body down, and tried to sleep. I lay awake, not moving, eyes open, staring upward at nothing, until the first colors of sunrise filtered through the Venetian blinds. Zombie-like, I got up, brushed my teeth, fed Tilly, and went outside into the cold morning air. In the yard grew a tall magnolia tree, its branches reaching heavenward, solid and black. Beneath it I prayed, 'Please, let Red be OK. Let me find her.' I DO NOT DESERVE THIS PUNISHMENT"; I screamed at the top of my lungs.

There was no answer.

I returned to the trailer house, took a sheet of paper from my sketchpad, and wrote:

Red,

I don't know what was going on last night. I have been looking for you. If you come home and find this note, I'll be back. We can straighten this out.

Love, Joseph

I tore off the sheet of paper from the tablet and taped it to the front door, in full sight, petted Tilly, got in the Pinto, and drove back to Lynchburg. I did not know where to begin to look. I started back at the 501 Club, and then drove out of town looking in every motel parking lot for Mac's van. North, south, east and west I drove. Every minute, every mile, driving me further into the deepest despair, I found nothing, not a trace. It was late in the afternoon when I finally gave up and returned home, worried and exhausted.

I pulled into the dirt driveway where Tilly was waiting, the nub of her tail wagging back and forth. I picked her up and walked to the door. There on top of the note I had taped to the door was Red's response, her elegant handwriting below my scribbled note. It said it all:

As Ronny Millsap says, "I wouldn't have missed it for the world." Gone to Ala-bama with Mac, Love, Red

Those words in her delicate feminine writing struck like a sledgehammer with the knowledge that I was a complete failure. My mother was right. I was worthless. I brought grief wherever I went, I would never amount to anything. I was a bastard. I was stupid; .And would become someone special when hell froze over.

I gave up as I looked at Red's note. I could go no further, and could endure no more.

I turned around, Tilly still in my arms and walked back to the Pinto. I got in and drove a quarter of a mile to my neighbor's house. Somehow I managed to get myself together long enough to leave Tilly with them.

"My wife left me," I explained. "So I'm going away and I can't take Tilly with me. Would you take care of her?"

I was friends with those neighbors and in particular, I admired the charming manners of the wife. Her name was Becky and she was a true child of the mountains. She sang like an angel and played the guitar. Her husband and I hunted turkeys and fished often together. Roy and I had shared a few good times. I knew they would take care of Tilly; they were honest, simple country people who made their living from a still.

I could feel myself coming apart as I stood there, dog in my arms. I put her down, returned to the still-running car, and drove off down the red dirt road, back to the highway that led to Lynchburg, Virginia.

A plan had formed in my mind. I was going to kill myself, no bullshit this time, no outs. I was going to do it with the Pinto and make it look like an accident. I did not want my children to bear the burden of a father who had blown his brains all over hell. Besides, I did not have a working gun.

Yes, I knew exactly what I was about to do. Just a short race from town was an overpass. It had two large support structures in the center of the highway. Those two towers of concrete and steel were going to be the final destination.

"Fuck God, Fuck all of you and to hell with it" I yelled, then pressed the accelerator to the floor. I was less than a mile away from the final moment on earth, both hands gripping the steering wheel as if welded to it. I was screaming at the top of my voice, not words, just piercing screams. I had my foot on the accelerator pressing it to the floorboards, the Pinto was going as fast as it possibly could, and tears were streaming down my face so freely I could hardly see to drive. Suddenly, the Pinto started to lose its forward movement. Seventy-five the speedometer read, then sixty, then fifty, I was screaming and crying. I stomped on the gas, the engine roared but the car continued to go slower. Finally, I saw it was hopeless and pulled the car off the highway as it rolled to a dead stop. By then, I had stopped screaming but my foot still had the accelerator pushed to the floor the engine was still roaring. The transmission was in drive yet the car remained motionless.

I killed the engine, stepped out of the car, pounded on the hood, then giving the door a hard kick, I screamed to the sky, "What are you doing to me now?"

If that fluid line to the transmission had not broken at that precise moment, in another 5 seconds I would have destroyed myself.

Leaving the Pinto where it had stopped, I walked the few miles back to the trailer house.

A bottle of French Brandy sat on the top of the refrigerator. It was full and I considered getting drunk, but instead of taking it down and opening it, I sat down at the drawing table and stared in a zombie-like trance. I may have stared that way for twenty minutes or twenty hours, I do not remember. I do not remember sleeping or eating.

I just sat reviewing my life, and those festers of shame that no one knew about. The corruption of my childhood, my humiliating academic and military career, my inability to stay at one employment, the awful and tragic marriage and divorce that left me bankrupt.

Every thing swept away. My mother's words, "I wish I never had you" reverberating in my ears.

Alone at the drawing table in that silent trailer house I wondered.

Who am I?

What am I?

The answer then came to me.

"You are Joseph, you are my creation."

"And what is my purpose for living?

"To be happy, to be proud of your self, to learn as much as you can while you are on this earth. This is your reason, this is your purpose."

Late Sunday evening I made a decision. I was going to continue learning to engrave. I was going to make myself a credit to the human race. I was going to Italy to study. My children needed me. I needed them. I was shattered and weak. I had to get well, strong again.

Chapter four

"MEMORIES IN THE SMOKE"

Monday morning early, I started walking back to Lynchburg and the Ken Hurst engraving company. It was very difficult to concentrate on the practice plate I was engraving. I had been making good progress until that fateful Saturday night at the 501 Club. With all that had happened, I could hardly work without the sadness, despair, and disappointment overwhelming me.

It was during this time that I decided to finish my high school education. I made an appointment for a GED (General Education Development) exam, which I passed without studying. Joseph was starting to feel a little bit better about his self. Somewhere I had bought a copy of a magazine called Omni. I liked it for its art layouts and interesting articles. The copy that I had read had an article in it featuring intelligence. "Test your IQ. How smart are you?"

The test consisted of several multiple-choice questions. I decided to fill out the questionnaire. While reading the questions and making the choices, I thought, 'This is really easy. I believe I have most of them right.' I waited anxiously for the next issue of Omni to come out. Meanwhile, continued to doing portraits at the Holiday Inn, the Hilton, shopping malls and various bars. The sketches were good and I would sometimes do three or four a night. I had gotten the Pinto repaired. The repairs cost less than $25. Finally came the day when I showed Mr. Hurst my most recent practice plate. He inspected it and pronounced it good enough for me to engrave professionally.

The next day Mr. Hurst gave me a weapon to engrave. It was a highly polished, Iver Johnson 9-shot revolver, costing the factory about $15 to produce and retailing at less than $100.

It was nothing more than a Saturday night special and a far cry from the beautiful custom shotguns that I admired featured in Signor Abbiatico's wonderful book.

Never the less, that cheap, ugly pistol was a milestone. I worried over the layout, sweated every stroke of the hammer, agonized over every cut the sharpened chisel made the entire day, while chasing the design into the steel. Finally, I was being paid (forty-eight dollars) to be an engraver. Any good engraver could have cut that design in less than two hours. It took me ten. I was not a good engraver; not even a mediocre engraver. I needed better teachers. I needed to go to Italy.

It was just about the time of my 42nd birthday that I quit working for Mr. Hurst, posted a sign at the crossroads country store saying that I was moving and was selling all that I owned. It was early next morning when a man in bib overalls drove a large green truck into the front yard.

"Ya'll the fellow that's selling out here?" He asked in a friendly good ole boy Virginia drawl.

"Yes, I am," I allowed.

"I came to see what ya'll get to sell."

He smiled, checked to see he had his wallet, and made his way up to the front door. I invited him in.

"I'm selling everything, I'm going to Italy." and told him to look at the furniture, pots, pans, stereo and anything else I owned including the Pinto.

We came to a cash price agreement. He backed the truck next to the door. There really was not much. The stove and the refrigerator belonged to the owner. Beds, linens, towels, records, stereo, tables, chairs, pots and pans, everything brought me $800. We were just about finished loading when the owner arrived at the scene.

"What's going on here?" he asked. "I was just down to the store and they said you were moving out."

"Yes, it's true; I'm going to Italy to become an engraver. My wife left me, so I'm free to go." I said knowing he would take no pity on me.

The property owner looked at me and said, "Well you ain't going nowhere until you settle the back rent you owe me Mister No Last Name."

The back rent was equal to what I had sold everything for. I pleaded with the property owner, "I need this money. I am going to Italy. I am going to become a successful engraver one day. And when I come back to the States I will pay you what I owe you." I argued to no avail.

"I'm calling the sheriff right now," he stated flatly. "The only place you're going is to the county jail."

When I heard the words, "county jail" I gave in. I would find another way.

"I'll tell you what," I said, "You give me fifteen minutes to gather up my personal things and you can have everything else that's here, including the car." I handed him the $800 dollars cash and the title to the Pinto. Then told the other fellow the deal was off .Went back into the trailer house, and pulled my clothes out of the closet. I selected shirts, socks, underwear and a couple of sweaters, stuffed them into a backpack I had purchased in anticipation of the trip to Italy along with my journal, sketchpad, drawing pen and some toiletries. Filled my pockets with the loose change I found lying around the place, picked up the engraving vise, packed it into a converted bowling ball bag, along with Magnivisor, hammers, and chisels.

Then took every scrap of paper that pertained to my life; divorce papers, marriage certificates, photos of my children, drawings, sketches, everything, carried the whole mess out the front door, put it in a pile, threw some kerosene on it and lit it.

Then stood there dry-eyed watching everything I had cared for and loved turn into smoking memories.

I put on the backpack, picked up the tool bag, and with no more conversation walked down the dirt road to my neighbor's house, where I asked him for a ride to town.

"Where do you want to go?" Roy asked.

I thought for a moment, trying to think of a reasonable answer to a reasonable question. Suddenly I realized that I was homeless, but it was unimportant. The trauma of trying to kill myself had in a very few days changed my entire outlook on life. I felt as all those sins, all those flaws had vanished. I was a different person. The edition of Omni finally came out and stated according to the test I had taken, I was a person with an IQ level of a genius, high enough to qualify me for Mensa Society.

I still remember thinking as I checked the score for the third time. If I am so smart, why was I so screwed up? This thought that I was not stupid, not worthless, was what I needed for morale at that moment in life. December of 1981 was when the seemingly unstoppable fall into the hell pit of life ended. I began to realize that I was indeed different, special, and unique. I started to like myself a bit better.

"I guess if you can give me a ride out to the 501 Club. That would be right kind of you," I finally answered the neighbor.

Why I said the 501 Club, I'm not sure. Perhaps it seemed to me that it was there life had, in one sense ended. Therefore, it seemed reasonable that perhaps it was at the 501 Club where I would discover where it began again.

As Roy was driving through town, I suddenly realized that I needed a place to store my tools and backpack.

"I need to swing by the bus depot for a couple of minutes Roy" He obliged me and pulled up to the curb out front.

At the bus depot, I rented a locker and left in it all the possessions I had in the world. How little I had left of all I had worked for. Wives, children, houses, cars, horses, cattle, furniture, hopes, and dreams, every thing gone, reduced down to a backpack and a bowling ball bag stuck in a Greyhound bus locker.

Chapter five

"LUCKY ME"

Here I was standing at the bar of the 501 club counting out pockets full of change and turning them into bills, at the same time trying to sell the barman a very good leather jacket. It was a nice jacket but was no protection from the cold. We were haggling over the price. He was offering me $20. I was asking $100.

"Gimme a break man., I paid $200 for this coat." I pleaded.

"I'll give you $20," was the barman's response.

"I need $40. I'm giving it away."

"Here's $25," said the barman. "Take it or leave it." I took it, stuck it in my wallet, and continued counting coins; I was still counting the change when another redhead stepped into my life.

"Did you win all that money playing poker? A feminine voice asked.

I stopped counting, grinned at the irony, then looked up into the brown eyes of a pleasant looking woman with medium length red hair; she was dressed in a pleated skirt, white blouse and was wearing sturdy white shoes.

"No," I replied. "This was my penny jar. I'm cashing it in for bills."

"Well, when you're done, come over and sit down with me and I'll buy you a beer."

She gave me a pretty smile and pointed to a booth by the wall. I looked at her more closely, trying to decide whether she was drunk or crazy.

Drawing people's portraits in a bad environment is a very enlightening experience; it gives the artist the time to look way down deep into people. I had been doing portraits for the better part of two years; I had met many screwed up people. Men very seldom wanted their portraits done unless the woman companion insisted to have it as a couple, or he was gay. It was always a woman who wanted me to do a sketch and she would be quite good-looking, slim, unable to control her nervous energy, and incapable of holding a pose for more than a couple of minutes. Most drank rum or vodka and fruit juices, most smoked, and were not

31

satisfied completely that I had captured their likeness on paper. All would take the sketch and show it to their friends.

"Is that me?" they would ask passing around the drawing. Everyone would nod or voice approval.

"Yep. Looks just like her," the audience would say. Finally, she would fish out my fee and ask me to sign the sketch.

As I studied this redhead, I did not see in her all of the warning signs saying that she was grief waiting to happen, even if I had, I made up my mind the minute she walked to the booth that I needed a place to sleep for the night. I finished business with the bar man then joined her in the booth "Hello" I said, as I slid into the opposite side. "My name is Joseph."

It was in Lynchburg that I had made friends with a local attorney. He knew my desire to go to Italy. He admired and respected that choice; He also had helped me with a social security card in the name of Joseph and a Virginia driver's license. Marshall was married and had two beautiful girls, five and eight years old, they were fascinated by the fact that I was named Joseph, and each time I saw them they would ask me "where is Mary?"

Late the next morning I walked over to Marshal William's office to talk to him about getting a passport, as I had not a clue what to do.

"You need an address, don't tell them you're homeless, use the address on your driver's license, that's first. A passport takes about two weeks to process but if you go directly to the agency you may be able to get it the next day." I thanked Marshall for his advice and help, we shook hands, and he wished me luck with my new adventure

My half-sister Ellen lived near Washington D.C. I had not talked with her in several months. Red and I had stopped to visit her on the way down to Lynchburg Virginia. We had spent a night visiting there. I called Ellen up and when she answered, explained to her that Red had left me and I needed a place to stay until my passport was ready.

"How long?" she asked.

I told her I couldn't tell for sure, at the most ten days. Her answer was, "Well gee, Joe. I don't know. I will first have to talk it over with Fred when he gets home. How do I get in touch with you?"

"Look Ellen, I'm at a pay phone in Lynchburg, Virginia. It is cold. I have no place to sleep and I'm almost out of money. How soon will it be before you talk to Fred?"

"Give me a number and I'll call you back in two hours." As I hung up, I thought. "Ellen you are Ernest's daughter of that I have no doubts."

It was very cold and I was not adequately dressed. Two hours standing in front of a public phone booth is a long, long time. Therefore, I decided to do some last minute shopping. I needed a warm coat and a few clothes. I had been considering writing a check on the now defunct account, how proud I had been of that checkbook with the single name on it. Having one name was unique but it also presented me with a multitude of problems. The checking account is an example, I recall the clerk who filled out the forms when I opened the new account saying, "You can't have, but one name, it's un-American," as she accepted the money.

I walked over to an Army-Navy store where I purchased a warm fleece-lined denim jacket, seaman's cap, a pair of wool gloves, two dress shirts, and a pair of Justin boots, then wrote the rubber check and left.

Now committed, I figured I might as well go all the way. I stashed the new shirts and boots at the bus depot. Put on the fleece lined new coat and gloves. Then walked to the Piggly Wiggly market, where I bought half a roasted chicken, a pint of vanilla ice cream, a handful of Snickers bars, some cigarettes, toothpaste, razor blades, and wrote another check. Taking them over to the city park, where I could sit down in the late afternoon sun, ate the chicken and ice cream, and then had a smoke while I waited for Ellen's call. Finally, the phone rang.

"Hello, hello, is that you Joe?"

"Ellen, who else could it be, what did Fred say, can I stay over?" I asked.

"Well, you know Joe. I talked it over with Fred and well, we really don't know you that well."

"Yes, well I love you too," I said as I hung up the phone.

January 1ˢᵗ, 1982 (From my diary)

A new year, a new lifestyle, Red is gone from my life forever. As for myself, I am now totally alone. My half sister who I thought cared for me has passed judgment on me and has decided I didn't fit in the normal world. I am alone but I am not truly alone.

I will be leaving Lynchburg in the next few days and going on to Italy. I am looking forward to my adventures there. I have just enough money for a one-way passage and food.

I am sure there will be many hard times ahead, although I believe the hardest are over. I have lived as honestly and truthfully, as I could, today I have decided to do something dishonest for money is extremely tight, I will need some clothes. I will write checks on the closed account to obtain them and will sell another man's property.

Dear Universal Spirit. Is there someone for me? A woman who will walk beside me? Are all people so afraid to leave their shelters, and chase their dreams, until they catch them? I do not believe I am wrong in my ideas and as one should trust one's own judgment, I shall continue to follow the route I have set out upon. I will climb my mountain. I will achieve my dreams, for this is what life is really about, Being yourself, believing in oneself and a Creator, just trying, that is all the human spirit can do.

I spent the last few hours in Lynchburg, Virginia saying goodbye to the engravers I had been working with and learning from: Tim, Ken, Carol, and John, each of the same mindset: artistic, independent, and seeking their own form of perfection. I have met some of them later in life. Each has become a great engraver. One outstanding engraver, John Robyn remembers me as an old man, he is twenty-five years my junior.

Waiting for the departure of the bus to take me to Hatborough Pennsylvania, I was determined to help my children. In addition, I was able to understand that I could never possibly help them in the precarious position that I was in.

First, I had to build a foundation, a foundation strong enough to support us when it came time to lift my children out of the craziness where I had abandoned them. I was a man who knew that he would excel, I was strong physically, but emotionally drained, a cloud of dispiriting, unrelenting, leaded fog had become draped around my shoulders. No matter how hard I tried, I could barely keep the sadness and tears at bay. Nevertheless, little by little, I was getting well. Almost unnoticeably at first, but slowly, I was transforming myself. The non-sufficient checks I had written troubled my conscience. As I waited for the bus, I bought postcards, which I sent to each of the stores:

Sometimes life seems to cause you to do things you regret. I will one day repay you.

Respectfully yours, Joseph

I put stamps on them and dropped them in a letterbox. The last thing I did before boarding the bus was to exchange the new Justin boots for the brogans that I had been wearing. I had not really needed those Justin boots, vanity caused me to buy them. Those brogans were completely comfortable, warm, and weatherproof, but I thought I would look better in cowboy boots. Sitting down on the bench across from the depot, I unlaced the perfectly good Browning field boots, took them off and placed them neatly under the bench, then slid on those cold, tight Justin's, lifted the backpack and tool bag, stepped up to the waiting bus and left Lynchburg Virginia, destination Jenkintown, Pennsylvania.

I had several friends in Jenkintown. A very dearest friend, Jim Tucker, was 15 years my junior. He was and still is a fine and meticulous stock maker. Jim had met and fallen in love with a beautiful woman who possessed the most enchanting personality. Her name is Evelyn, but everyone called her Ev.

It was late evening when I showed up at Jim and Ev's apartment in Jenkintown. After explaining my situation, they gladly let me spend the night on their sofa. Jim and Ev later married and had a son, whom, to my great honor they gave the name of Joseph.

The following morning with hugs, kisses and farewell wishes, I made the train trip from Jenkintown to Hatborough, where there were other friends, including the lawyer Mr. Gold, who had done the legal work to change my name. I was sure I could find someone to stay with at the Red Barn apartments. I was not as concerned about a roof over the head as I was about money; I had already the bad checks in Lynchburg on my conscience. Joseph was not very proud of himself but he was determined and determination meant doing what you had to do to succeed. I had a good friend and customer when I was a gunsmith. His name is Don Moran.

Don was a good appreciative customer. Not long before I began the quest to become an engraver, he had left with me a very nice antique rifle for repair and restoration. I had not finished it when I closed my shop and went down to Jenkintown to work for the Paul Jaeger Co. I had contacted Don and explained to him the situation. His answer was, "Take it with you to Pennsylvania and when you finish it, UPS it back to me." I had sold all my gunsmith tools and I could not take the rifle to Italy, I could have sent it back to my trusting friend. Instead, I sold it along with my tools in Lynchburg.

When I sold Don's gun and pocketed the cash, I was in a very sorry state, and I had developed a sty on my right eyelid. Something I had not experienced before "Great, I said out loud as I studied the lesion in the mirror "I am going blind."

At the rate money was flowing out of my pocket, I was concerned that there would not be enough for airfare. Pennsylvania was very cold, wet snow was still falling. The Justin boots chafed my ankles raw, they were slick-soled, and I fell several times on the icy sidewalks ending up in the snow-filled gutters of Jenkintown. In despair, I took them to a cobbler and had those bloody cursed boots stretched, it did no good … I recall saying to myself as I slipped and slid around Hatborough …, "I deserve this; God is punishing me for stealing." With every twinge, I would wince and think, "I deserve this."

I settled in with one of my friends from the Red Barn apartments. He is gay which did not bother me because I love/hate women, besides, the pain and trauma of childhood rape removes a great many temptations.

At the first opportunity I found the U.S. passport agency, filled out the required forms, handed them back to a fat, angry, authoritative woman and then sat back to wait for the issuing of my passport. It was not long before she looked at me, then the application, then scowled and pointed at me, and then with her ring laden fingers beckoned me over to her window.

"You didn't put down your last name"

"No ma'am, that's my full legal name," I replied.

"Do you have proof?" She asked.

"Yes ma'am," I answered.

"Well, let me see it, and for your sake I sure hope you have a lot."

I produced the court order, Virginia driver's license, and social security card. She grabbed them up and disappeared into her supervisor's office. After a long, anxious wait she returned, frowned then said

"Only in America"

I smiled, looked at her closely and whispered, "Isn't it great"

She broke into the widest grin, accepted the passport photo, took the money, punched, stamped, and finally handed me a passport. Saying as she did "Here you are Mister Joseph, have a nice vacation." I became completely legitimate.

I had met a friendly man at the local bar in Hatborough. This was before I had a passport. We got to talking about hunting; this led to the topics of guns, which of course led to my illustrious engraving career. He had a pistol he wanted engraved. I had the tools but no place to work. He suggested I work on his pistol at his home. We struck a quick bargain. He would provide me with room and board, while I engraved his Ruger .44 magnum. I would get some much-needed cash. Quickly I moved out of the Red Barn and started working on my very first engraving commission. I wish I could remember his and his wife's name and once again thank them for all the kindness that they showered on me during the days I struggled with that super hardened steel that Mr. Ruger puts in his guns. I remember the work I did. It was amateurish and poorly cut, but he was happy with it. He insisted that I sign it, so I engraved "J" near the trigger guard, and as I did, the chisel slipped, cutting a large gouge across the polished surface. With great embarrassment, I showed him the slip. He thought it was just great. As far as he was concerned, it made his Ruger a valuable collector's item. He gladly paid me.

Some one Listens

One day I came into my friend's apartment, and God, who had been watching my struggles, reached down and touched me.

Chapter six

"THE ROAD TO ITALY"

The time had finally arrived to buy a ticket to Italy so I set forth with the newly acquired passport, made my way by railway to Kennedy International.; I had absolutely no idea of what to do, the only thing I knew was that I had to go to Italy. I had never flown on a commercial airline. Did not even know that Italy had more than one airport. I had no idea that you had to make reservations in advance, or what a ticket cost. Somehow, I made it to New York, and the same airport I had picked up my French bride from, twenty years earlier.

I was a country boy, and a country boy can make himself comfortable most anywhere except in the middle of a city. The airport was a huge city as far as I was concerned. I found the international flight counters for foreign lands. Then would stand in line and when it came time, ask the cost of a ticket to Italy.

"Where Sir, in Italy would you like to go? A clerk would ask "What city there are you going to visit?"

I could not pronounce the name of my destination, when the clerk would ask. I would show them the envelope with the address on it. "Here," I would say, "is where I want to go, Gardone, Val Trompia, it is located in Italy"

Nobody seemed to be able to find Gardone or Brescia. Eventually, Milan came up has a final destination. I do not recall the ticket prices but they were way out of my budget. I tried them all, airline after airline, I tried a one-way ticket, Still too much money, I tried Air France hoping it would be cheaper, no monsieur! I finally ended up at Laker Airlines. They did not fly to Italy only to London.

"How much is a ticket?" I asked.

"$408 roundtrip."

"And one-way? "I asked again.

"$204."

"The next available seat sir, is this Wednesday."

It was three days away, I decided to buy the ticket then and sleep and eat in the airport until the flight's departure for Heathrow Airport, London, England.

"I'll buy a ticket please." I smiled at the clerk, got out my wallet, passport and paid cash for it.

During the second day of waiting for the flight, I met a man who helped change my life forever. He was trim, fit, and not much older than I was. He was casually dressed in black slacks and white shirt, carrying a heavy tan coat over one arm, in his other hand, he held a worn leather satchel … He happened to sit down next to me.

"How are you?" he asked.

I did not respond, for I was deep into my past.

"Is some one occupying this seat?" he asked again.

I answered "no."

He quickly made himself comfortable, sighed, and absently said.

"I have such a long way to travel; I am going all the way to Calcutta, India"

Surprised, I said, "from the little that I know, it is a very poor place to live."

"One gets used to it" he replied.

I was curious; I asked him what he did in Calcutta.

"I am a missionary and have been for 10 years now; I am in charge of six thousand poor who look to me for care and hope."

I finally looked directly at him, studying him, trying to decide if I believed him.

I said, "That must be very difficult to see, all those poor, sick people whose lives have been so abused"

"Yes, yes it is, it's very difficult, and that is why I am there, for the need of my help." He said softly.

My curiosity was aroused. "How can you help so many people?"

He replied, "I talk to each one of them, I get them to ask for help in sharing the secret fears they carry in their minds."

"And this helps them?" I asked.

"Absolutely, for once a secret is told it's no longer a burden, and once a fear is revealed, it disappears."

I did not respond but resumed thinking while he opened his satchel, retrieved a small black book, and began to read its pages.

As I reflected in solitude, I remembered my darkest of darkest secrets. I considered them silently while the man studied his small black book.

I realized that I would never see this man again and thought. He does not know me; the secrets I carry keep eating my life away. I want to be rid of them. I inhaled, let out a ragged sigh, and then told him how my great- uncle Andrew had terrorized me as a child.

"It was in the dairy barn" I began "behind the large wooden barn doors that he grabbed me, he placed his huge hand on my shoulder.

"Would you like ten cents," he asked, showing me a shiny small coin.

To a boy of six it was a small fortune. He reached into his bib over-alls and pulled out his pecker. "Lick this and I will give you this dime."

"Give me the dime first," I said, for I did not trust Uncle Andrew. He gave me the dime saying,

"I got a good hold of you boy" as he gripped my arm.

Suddenly he grabbed my head and forced himself into my mouth. It hurt terribly and I started to gag. I struggled but could not get away, he had a hand full of my hair, I felt vomit rise in my throat. Andrew let me go, the churning mass in my throat spewed forth, the filthy taste is something that the thought of, still makes me sick now, even after all those years.

I stopped speaking, trying to recover my composure, inhaled, let my breath out, and continued.

I broke free of him, ran across the barnyard to the farmhouse, Andrew behind me. I flew up the stone steps into the kitchen with tears streaming down my face. I told great-aunt Lillian what had happened, what I had done; Andrew had entered the kitchen at that point. She accused him; he called me a lying bastard. I showed her the dime I still had in my hand.

She grabbed the nearest thing handy and threw it at him saying, "Do not touch this child again" It was his coffee mug and it hit him in the head. He went out the door and never touched me again."

As soon as I said it I felt cleansed, the ugly shame had dissolved. The man got up from his seat, shook my hand and said, "I am sure God has his plans for you"

He handed the small black book, "I have underlined some passages for you to read, I must go now, my flight is boarding."

We shook hands again; I thanked him for the book and his kindness, and then watched as he walked swiftly down the corridor and out of my life. After he left, I opened his book, and began to read.

"My Dearest Joseph,

I know it is not by mere accident in life that we have met today. I truly believe God brought me all the way from my mission in Calcutta India and I know He will give you the desires of your heart.

I longed to be used by Him. To help the children of India; I never dreamed I would have 6,500 in school today, "The secret, page 49" Your friend Math XXXX.

The Secret

I met God in the morning, when the day was at its best.
   All day the Presence lingered, All day long He stayed with me.
   And we sailed in perfect calmness over a very troubled sea.
   Other ships were torn and battered, other ships were sore distressed. But the winds that seemed to drive them, Brought to us a peace and rest.
   Then I thought of other mornings, with a keen remorse of mind,
   When I to had loosed the moorings, With the Presence left behind.
   So, I think I know the secret, learned from many a troubled way. You must seek Him in the morning. If you want Him through the day.

                                          _ R.S.C.

(See author's notes)

Finally came the moment when I checked the backpack, tools, and engraver's vise. The vise was compact enough that you could hold it in both hands. It was a 9-inch block of solid chromium steel weighing thirty-five pounds. Carrying it had been difficult, it was a great relief to hand it and backpack over to the baggage clerk. When asked to put a nametag on the luggage, I pondered for a moment, and then wrote in my finest script, "Joseph." then put the tags on the backpack and bowling ball bag, gratefully handed them to the attendant; he reached for the bag and grunted in surprise at its weight.

"What on earth is in there?" He wanted to know.

I replied, "My tools, open it up if you like, it's not locked."

I would rather that you do that sir," he said handing me back the bag.

Once relieved of my baggage I went into the men's lounge, freshened up, returned to the departure area, and made myself comfortable.

I had not been able to sleep for the last two nights, part anxiety, and part excitement. Now, while waiting for the boarding call I could hardly keep my eyes from closing. I remember finally getting on board and finding a seat.

The next thing I recall is standing in the immigration and custom line in Heathrow Airport. People were speaking in English but no one spoke as I did.

Dazed and confused, I found my luggage, passed through customs without a hint of problems, got on a bus and later found myself walking down some busy street in London, feeling very hungry.

The bag containing the vise maintained its torturous gravitational pull on my fingers, wrist, arms, and shoulders. I would carry it for a while in one hand and then switch the weight to the other for respite of my aching muscles. The sty had disappeared, but the boots continued to torture my ankles.

Suddenly a stranger stops me and asks, "What are you carrying in the bag? It looks very heavy."

I stopped and started telling him, a complete stranger, a small part of my life story. How I was going to Italy, where I intended to learn engraving, how tired, and hungry I was. He listened, and then he offered to carry part of the weight of tool bag.

"Let me give you a hand mate, I know my way around this city as well as I know the back of my hand," he said.

He was going to show me where I could find cheap accommodations. I was looking for a YMCA. He explained that there were cheaper places further along the street. He helped me carry the vise a block or so. I was so grateful for the relief I offered to buy breakfast. We went into a restaurant where I ordered bacon, eggs, hash browns, and coffee for both of us. The food arrived. It was delicious. I ate ravenously.

During the meal, my newfound friend told me he was a truck driver. In fact, He had a truckload of fish he was taking over to France and then was continuing on to Spain from there. He talked about Dover England, sea link ferries, the truckers that hauled freight to France and the rest of Europe. He said he was in the process of fueling up his truck and should be ready to leave in about one hour. I asked if he would give me a lift. He cheerfully agreed to do so. He said he had a few errands to run and needed to change some English pounds into francs, refuel his truck, and then buy some whiskey to bribe the French customs guards. I was so tired I could not think straight, I could go no further. I had $50 in British currency. I said to my new friend,

"Would you take this money and change into francs for me. I'll just sit here and rest until you return." With smiles and promises, he took the money and put it in his pocket.

"I'll be back in an hour, sit tight and don't worry mate." About four hours later, I understood he was not going to return. I have never trusted anyone who has recently made my acquaintance and calls me friend since that day.

The loss of the cash was crucial. All I had left was enough to purchase a $204 ticket back to New York. Discouraged, I walked down the darkening street looking for a place to spend the night. I eventually found a place managed by a sweet old lady, it was obvious at first glance, that she ran a clean, tidy bed and breakfast. She charged me $10 for a room that included a bit to eat that evening, and breakfast the next morning.

That night for the first time in a long time, I cried again. In that small, cold dark room in Jolly Old England, I sat and I cried, silently and strongly.

"What should I do? Give up? Return to Jaegers? Return to the states and find work? I thought for a long while, and then I realized if I failed here, I had proved absolutely nothing. My journal would be nothing but meaningless empty words.

"I am someone special," I thought. "God loves me."

I had time to think over what the truck driver had said. If I could get to Dover, I could then catch the ferry to Calais. He had told me also that if you were in a vehicle, only the vehicle was charged passage, but if you were a passenger, you would pay $35. I decided to go for it. From my journal:

January 17th, 1982
Dear Universal Mind
Thank you for giving me such good fortune. I will not fail you, nor break my promises to you.

The next morning, I awoke revitalized and was once again in good spirits. After a small breakfast, I asked the proprietor for directions to the bus and train terminals, and then thanked her for her kindness. She then kissed me on the cheek, like a mother seeing her child off to school, and like a child on his first day of school, I put on coat, watch cap, and gloves, adjusted the backpack, hefted the bowling ball bag, and stepped out into the cold and fog of London town ...

My luck had begun to change. The railway station was but a short distance from that friendly B&B. Quickly, I found passage on the train that ran to Dover, with its famous white cliffs. Across the gray-green, southeast part of England rolled the train, while I watched the landscapes pass by the window. One of the passengers in the compartment was a young, pretty girl. I passed the time flirting with her a bit, while doing a quick sketch of her profile. The ride to Dover was of very short duration.

Once off the train I settled the backpack on my shoulders, picked the tool bag up off the platform then walked to its end, trying to find the pier. I could see the ferry in the distance. The thing was huge! Its size was dumbfounding; it was maybe three football fields long, and equally one wide. There was an enormous ramp at the stern were you could see trucks queued up waiting to board, truck after semi- truck, full of freight all bound for the far corners of Europe. There were a few cars also, but mostly trailer trucks.

I had arrived again by providence, about two hours before departure.

I decided to try to hitchhike onto the ferry to avoid the fare

For the next hour I stood just outside the ramp with thumb stuck in the air, finally the whistle for departure started bellowing. I took my baggage, walked up the giant ramp, paid the fare, and found the way into the passenger's lounge.

Italy was now only 400 miles away, or three thousand miles closer, depending on your point of view.

The passenger's lounge was full of young tough men, all truckers, talking in languages I did not understand. They were Frenchmen, Greeks, Spaniards, Germans, Slavs, Englishmen, and Italians, all with cargo to deliver throughout Europe. These men were far from their homes as well, and I easily made their acquaintance.

I soon had explained my situation to one of them in my rusty half forgotten French. (A language learned from my first wife) He then in turn took me to another group of truckers where they questioned me and asked for identification. They wanted to see my identification, tools, and belongings; they were a very wary group of men, who lived a dangerous life.

After it was determined that I was not a criminal, or a terrorist, about a dozen of them started buying me drinks and food. Then one of them explained to me, they had found a trucker that was going to Milan. They had arranged it with him for me to ride in that truck and over beers introduced me to the driver. He was a stout man about 30 years of age; he spoke not a word of English or French. He had a badly pockmarked face and someone's fist had flattened his nose at some point in his life. He was warmly dressed in woolen pants, shirt, and jacket.

I shook his hand and could immediately feel the strength of his calloused grip. I returned his handshake with equal strength. We looked each other straight in the eyes, smiled, nodded, and then resumed drinking in silence.

The time I had been waiting for finally came; soon I would be on my way through France. I followed the trucker down the spiral steel staircase, Those Justin boots clanking as we descended into the parking areas of the ferry. Huge diesel trucks covered with heavy dirty tarps sat row after row, all in silence ... Soon all those motors would whine, spit, and roar to life. Engines would idle, warming the frozen horsepower that was to carry me through France and into Italy.

God had sent many angels to help on this journey and I thanked him as I climbed up in the cab, if not for the London thief I most likely would have failed. I settled the fact that the $50 he had taken was worth every penny for the information he had provided.

Francisco, the Italian trucker, was to become my patron saint. As the kilometers rolled on, I would ask him questions, 'What is this?' pointing to my ear or pointing to my nose. 'Or this?' pointing to the steering wheel. I knew I had to learn some of the Italian language, if I were to survive. Francisco would not allow me to pay one franc during the whole trip.

That night we stayed in a small village with a trucker's restaurant and bar. The barmaids were flirtatious and I began to recover some of my French tongue and could converse quite well. The bar girls bought me dinner and drinks; I did their portraits in return. That night, I slept deep and well. Morning coffee with milk and sugar accompanied baguettes of fresh bread, fresh marmalade, strawberries, and butter. Soon, we were back onto the freightliner and on the road, we went. Again, he did not allow me to pay.

The second day of traveling ended late that afternoon. The countryside of France had gone from farmland with drizzling skies to a grinding uphill climb with bitter cold, snow, and ice. The weather continued to worsen, we pulled to the roadside where I helped Francisco chain up. The weather was nasty, and getting nastier by the moment. It was turning dark when we pulled into the customhouse on Mont Blanc, dividing France from Italy. Mont Blanc more than lived up to its name. Francisco placed the freightliner in neutral, set the brakes then we chocked the wheels, checked the tires, and went into a small concrete building for coffee.

There was a blazing fire in a cast iron wood stove and the heat felt most luxurious compared to the insufficient heater in the truck. Since the first moment I had put those Justin boots on my feet, they were either cold or freezing. They had chafed my shinbones raw, yet with every twinge, I would think, "you deserve it."

It was with great reluctance that I left the warmth of the cast iron stove and headed back to the truck, where I would sleep for the next two nights. To say I damn near froze my testicles off would be an accurate description.

The moon was full, its light flooding the parking area. There was no electricity, although I could see the tops of cables strung on power poles sticking barely over the drifting snow. These were not the little knee-high snowdrifts I had crashed through as a child, on great-aunt Lillian's dairy farm. These drifts were as high as a two-story house. Francisco pulled out his wool blanket and pillow and crawled into the sleeping compartment, Soon he was snoring loudly.

I continued to sit in the passenger seat wearing all the clothes I had, four shirts, pullover sweater, wrangler jacket buttoned to the throat with the collar turned up, I had my watch cap pulled over my ears, gloves on and my arms wrapped tightly around myself. Still, I could feel the warmth seeping from my body. I slept not a bit all night. It was so cold. I got out my sketchpad and drew the whole moonlit scene with icy trembling hands. I drew the ice, the trucks, the snow, trying to keep my mind off my freezing feet.

The sun rose and daylight spread its warming glow over the border crossing on Mont Blanc. I tried to understand why we were not continuing on to Milan but the language barrier prevented that. Finally, the coffee shop opened its doors. I stumbled out of the truck and into the blessed warmth of the cast iron stove. Francisco continued to snore peacefully for another hour.

The journey ended on January 20, on a snowy cold, exhausting, late afternoon … With a hiss of airbrakes, I stepped down from the cab, gathered up the bowling ball bag and backpack, waved to the smiling driver, and looked at the new surroundings. I had managed to transport myself into a completely different world.

From my journal:
Italy New York- London$204   *Room in London: $10*
    Money Lost: $50   *Money Spent $12*
    Fare to France: $35   *Fare to Milan: $0*
            Money Spent in France: $20
Arrived in Gardone, Val Trompia, and Italy with $190 cash, left in my wallet
Dear Universal Mind,
    Please keep me safe and find a way to survive. I am so alone and so afraid. Not afraid of harm, but that I will not have the funds to be able to stay here.

Chapter seven

"ARRIVAL IN GARDONE VAL TROMPIA"

The town looked old and solid, cobblestone streets were worn smooth from the whizzing traffic, cars flying past, people on bicycles, motor bicycles, on foot. Everyone was busy. Everyone seemed to be dashing about on this or that errand and no one spoke English. It had taken only seven days to make the trip.

Across the street from where I stood, was a bookshop; I made my way across the traffic and into the bibliotheca and bought a small Italian-English dictionary.

With the dictionary open to the phrase "cheap hotel," I walked up to a man wearing a uniform, I thought he might have been the police, and then showed him the phrase. He looked it over then beckoned me to follow him. He walked up a steep stone walkway that was shaded by ancient chestnut trees to the principal town square, then took me to a bar/restaurant, introduced me to the owner and in a short time I was in a comfortable room with soft clean sheets and a mattress.

I stripped off my road-grimed clothes, sweated, and strained until I had those damn boots off, took a hot bath, and slept like the dead until late the next day.

The owner of the Albergo in Gardone was exactly what you would imagine; short in stature, long on warmth, and welcoming in kindness. He spoke a little French, between that and my dictionary; I was able to make myself understood. My biggest problem was to understand him. He spoke rapidly, leaving me clueless as to what he said. I believe, he thought I was a wealthy eccentric tourist or perhaps a journalist for one of the many sporting magazines that came to Gardone, Val Trompia to review the precious arms collections housed in the Beretta Firearms Museum, and meet the engravers whose work attracts worldwide attention.

If your interests were art, engraving, or the finest quality rifles and shotguns in the world, the small village of Gardone Val Trompia founded centuries before along the trout-filled Mella River, is the greatest Mecca on earth. And, I was there. Now, all I had to do was hang on, I was nearly broke, in pain and I was lonely. I carried a gaping hole in my soul from the loss of my children. I seemed to be unable to shake my depression.

I had made up my mind that I would never again allow another woman to come close to my heart; I would flirt or seduce but never, ever, again trust another female. I just could not accept more pain. Now that I had freed myself of forty-odd years of looking for a mother's breast to suckle, I had not intention of falling in that tender trap, again. No, sir, No thank you, ma'am, I'd been there and I'd done that.

My goal when I arrived in Gardone, Val Trompia was to learn engraving, while earning money as a gunsmith on a part-time basis. The whole trip was based on the fact that once in Italy, I would find work. Some of the tools I carried to Italy I had made at Jaeger's, they were for woodworking. I had made them with pride, and expected that they would be good examples of my skills.

The next morning, feeling rested and excited, I started the day with this entry in my journal:

I will become a master engraver by April 20th, 1982.

I certainly did overestimate myself. With this attitude, I set forth from the Albergo Hotel Gardone … Bathed, shaved, and neatly dressed, wearing those good-looking boots, I stepped out into the cold, polluted, morning sunlight of Gardone Italy.

Gardone resembled no place I had ever seen, its streets were narrow, wide enough for horse carts, motorbikes, pedestrians, cats, dogs, and rats. A large canal of swiftly moving water flowed half the town's length providing power to the gun companies of Gardone. Soot coated everything, from the steel mills and manufacturing plants. Machinists, gun makers, stock makers, barrel makers and engravers, all working in unison to produce the most beautiful firearms in the world. In the pocket of my denim jacket, I had the ragged letter with the return address of Signor Abbiatico.

I walked up the one main road looking for a street sign. Most streets had none, and if there was one, I could not read it. I stopped at a bar, bars opened very early in the mountainous country of Italy, pointed at a croissant, and asked for coffee. Coffee is a word pronounced similarly in most of the world's languages. The barmaid looked at me curiously then asked "Corretto o Cappuccino?" Not sure what she had asked, I nodded my head in the affirmative.

Fortune once more intervened in my favor. I tasted my first cappuccino. Refreshed and enthusiastic, I continued to walk up the street. Florists, butcher, hardware shops, and tobacconists—all were open. The air was sharp but not sub-freezing; the breeze carried the odor of sewer. Piles of dirty snow and grime were everywhere. Gardone in January was not a very pretty picture.

Suddenly, there in the window of a photo shop, was what I had been searching after. There, prominently displayed was an enlargement of the underside of a Famars made-shotgun receiver. The engraving had been enlarged ten times its actual size. The scene depicted was of Diana the huntress; bow in hand, hands at her naked thighs, arrows in her quiver, the antelope she had just shot lying on the ground. The engraver had cut every detail of the trees, rocks, skies into the precious steel. As soon as I saw that photo, I rushed into the shop.

"Where is that? Where is that?" I asked.

Not understanding the question the owner went outside to see at what I was pointing. Now it became clear to him what I wanted, he summoned a small boy from the back, gave him instructions, and then indicated that I should follow the boy.

One street past the photo shop, walk until you come to a small triangular park with a clear running stream bisecting it, cross over the ancient Roman footbridge, walk a half a block, look to the left, and you will find yourself in front of the villa of Abbiatico& Salvinelli.

The boy turned into the elegant courtyard, went up to the office, and rang the bell. Promptly Signor Abbiatico's secretary appeared. She spoke to the boy then looked at me, then motioned me into the office. I had arrived at my destination. Signor Abbiatico stood up from his desk and offered his hand. I believe that, at that moment he assumed I was a rich American client. I handed him his letter, explaining to him that I had indeed finished art school and, learned how to engrave, showing him the practice plate I had brought all the way from Virginia as I did so. I was now ready to work for him learning to engrave. Mario spoke excellent English; he asked me how I arrived. I said simply, I had hitchhiked.

"You have made a very long trip for nothing," he said. "I couldn't provide you with work no matter what your skills, I am not an engraver. I am the author of a book on engraving, but I am not an engraver."

I could feel myself disintegrating. Before I could say anything he continued, "There is a school here that teaches engraving. Let me make a phone call."

After a brief conversation, Signor Abbiatico replaced the phone, looked at me, and said, "Signor Giovanelli will see you at his office at noon. Please come to my office a few minutes before so I may take you there."

With that, his secretary showed me out. With nearly three hours to wait; I returned to the Albergo and using the newly purchased dictionary composed a note. In it, I expressed my desires to learn to engrave and said it was my dream to come to Italy to study.

Around 11:30, I retraced my steps back to Famars gun works to find Signor Abbiatico. We got in his car and drove up the narrow one-way road that led to the town of Magno. The total distance was a good hour's walk from my hotel. We arrived at the Bottega d' Incisione di Giovanelli promptly and were shown into Signor Giovanelli's office by a strikingly beautiful woman, Signor Giovanelli's secretary.

Signor Giovanelli was a very elegant man, his office impeccably furnished in black leather and chrome furniture. On prominent display were sculptures of marble and bronze, several two-foot by three-foot framed enlargements of engraved Beretta shotguns hang on the walls along with original drawings and paintings.

Signor Giovanelli was everything I had never been or dreamed of becoming. He was rich, tall, handsome, had three beautiful daughters, one of which was learning the engraving trade. Maria Giovanelli was 16 years old; her father was one year younger than I was. Signor Giovanelli had a mountain villa for a home, traveled the world first-class, and owned several other companies, luxury autos, even a helicopter. He was the first truly wealthy person I had met.

His school was the main provider of engraving services to Colt, Winchester, Smith and Wesson and most importantly, Beretta.

Cesare Giovanelli himself was not an engraver. He was more than an engraver. He was the artist patron. Every part of the building that housed his pleasures showed his love of art and beauty He had secured the services of an interpreter for our meeting. Signor Abbiatico introduced me and kindly ordered me to sit. I felt as if I were in audience with a prince or perhaps a count. I felt as if I was standing in an imaginary castle, standing at the door of my personal heaven, and Signor Giovanelli was the gatekeeper.

I handed him the note that I had written. It said:

Dear Sir,
I have come to Italy in pursuit of my dreams of learning to engrave.

Most respectfully yours
Joseph

Mr. Giovanelli took his time to read the note, and then asked through the interpreter how did I get there …

"I hitchhiked." I answered,

My heartbeat rapidly increased as the interpreter asked to present my identification, which I promptly did. Then he began to question the fact that the passport said Joseph and nothing else. I explained it by saying that I was an orphan and knew neither my mother nor my father.

"How long do you intend to stay?"

"Until I learn," I answered.

"How much money do you have?"

"Sir, I have one hundred and forty seven dollars"

"How will you support yourself? The school cannot give you employment."

"I can take care of myself," I replied, after a few more questions. The interpreter asked me to go outside and wait on the terraced courtyard. I walked outside across the grey cobblestones, past the sculptures in marble, bronze, and welded steel. From the end of the terrace, you could see down the length of the entire valley, far below lay the red tile roofs of the town Gardone Val Trompia. I found a place to sit in the sun for it was cold and windy, once I was comfortable I began to pray.

A half hour had passed when the secretary came back for me. She escorted me back into Signor Giovanelli's office.

The interpreter then said, "Signor Giovanelli has decided to accept you into his school, he would like you to go out to the engraving room and cut a steel plate so that he may judge at what level of competency you are."

Taking my tool bag, I followed Signor Giovanelli into the engraving room. It was such a sharp contrast to Mr. Hearst's company that I became very confused and nervous, everything was neat and orderly, each of the twenty engravers had their workstations placed directly in front of a plate glass window, which flooded the entire long, tiled floor room with indirect north light. Signor Giovanelli accompanied me to the workstation of the Maestro, where the interpreter introduced us. The Maestro was a thin, intense, bearded man wearing eyeglasses with pink tinted lenses, Renato Sanzogni. The adjacent work station was cleared and a brightly polished block of steel 6 inches long, 2 inches wide and 2 inches thick was placed in the floor mounted, rotating, engravers vise. I opened my tool bag to remove Magnivisor, hammer and chisel, the Maestro staid my hand as I went to place the magnifier on my head, he then spoke rapidly to the interpreter as he examined my chisel, its point, and my hammer.

The interpreter said, "The Maestro says that you cannot use the magnifying device and that your tools are not good."

The maestro handed me a small fragile chisel and a tiny hammer weighing about 2 ounces. Signor Giovanelli then spoke to the interpreter and the Maestro. The Maestro then shook my hand, took a compass and scribed several lines on the steel block placed it in the vise, then the interpreter said,

"The Maestro would like you to cut these lines

Everything was unfamiliar, from the way they held the tools, to the type of vise they worked with. I was at a loss without magnification to see the work; I tried to cut a straight line on the plate, but failed miserably.

After the demonstration that I was completely without skill, we returned to the office.

Signor Giovanelli wants to know. "When would you like to begin school?" the interpreter asked.

I answered, "Tomorrow."

"Forget all you have learned in the States, that it completely wrong, your tools are unnecessary. The school will provide the tools you need; a very small hammer, chisel, chalk, pencil, and a compass." With that, Signor Giovanelli dismissed me and Sig. Abbiatico, who had attended the entire interview, gave me a ride back down the mountain. I thanked Mario for his kindness and entered the hotel to wait impatiently for the next morning.

January 20th, 1982 (From my journal)

I have been accepted. Signor Giovanelli has accepted me into his school of engraving. There I will become a master engraver. I have suffered much to arrive at this plateau in my life. I suppose that the loneliness and hard effort will continue until I achieve success. I am no fool. I know that once I achieve success, many people will want to be close to me.

Please, help me … I love you. I work for you.

Am I not entitled to some contentment, someone to share with me my dream? To be alone is very hard for me to bear.

Your creation, Joseph

The next morning I got up early and used the clean communal shower down the hall from my second floor accommodations, hungrily I ate the fruit bought at the fruit stand the day before. The Albergo bar was open and doing brisk business at 7 a.m. The owner's wife was behind the bar fixing espresso coffee and serving shots of brandy or grappa to the workers, most of whom worked for Beretta.

"Come have coffee and a brioche or a sandwich' she said to me, with a kindly smile

I accepted espresso coffee; it was rich, black, and full of flavor and tasted nothing like the weak, instant coffee that I was accustomed to drinking.

Fortified with enough caffeine to increase my heartbeat, I headed off for the first day of school. I had decided that the only possible way to survive was accept no charity. I would not ask for food, money, or help, I would earn money somehow. As I made the hour-long hike through Gardone and up the mountainside to the town of Magno and Signor Giovanelli's school, I wondered how I would survive. I had to find a job; I needed to make some money. I decided to do portraits after school. I was sure I could find a way.

January 23, 1982 (From my journal)

Engraving school is wonderful. Six hours of design and drawing lessons a week. Hours and hours of cutting smaller and smaller circles on practice plates, everyone is nice to me. I know with perspiration, perseverance, and patience I will master this art of engraving. Loneliness and cold are my biggest enemies. Somehow, they seem to go hand in hand. Maybe someday it will all be worthwhile. Look after me.

Chapter eight

"LEARNING THE STROKES"

Engraving school left little time to think and rehash in my mind what I could have done differently for my children's sake. Slowly, I started to come out of my depression; I felt my spirits starting to lift again. I became totally absorbed in school. I had the world's finest teachers. Signor Giovanelli put me under the direct supervision of Maestro Renato Sanzogni, the thin, bearded, redheaded man, who was fifteen years my junior. Renato worked directly on my right, he taught me how to hold the chisel and hammer properly, how to stand correctly in front of the vise, and how to make a handheld graver cut steel with surgical precision. I was doing well with the Italian language, and was making progress learning how to use the small, delicate, chasing hammer.

The first thing I had to learn was to be able to make a solid contact with the hammer face against the chisel. Every stroke had to be precise or the delicate point of the engraving chisel would break. Once the point was broken it would no longer cut properly and would have to be re-sharpened, a process done under 6-power magnification and could take a novice up to thirty minutes to complete.

It was three months before I learned to make a perfect stroke with the hammerhead against the graver. The beginning was agony, I would swing the hammer twice and the point would break, I would have to re-sharpen. Day after day, I would stand in front of that vise, seven hours a day, five and a half day a week, trying to connect with the end of the chisel without looking at the hammer fall.

After three weeks of continuous practice, I could cut a semi-straight line three inches long in a steel practice block. Line after line, each equal thickness, and width apart, I cut on the practice block. When its surface was covered I would show it to the Maestro, he would examine it, send it to the machine shop where the work was milled off, and the clean block then brought back. I would place it in the vise, polish the block to a smooth luster, and then begin filling it again with fine lines. I stood on that stone tile floor of the engraving room, cutting line after line until I could do it with absolute precision, standing in those god-damned boots, day after day while the arches of my feet begged for relief from the pain caused by standing in one spot for such long periods ...

January 26th, 1982
To Whom It May Concern, I have been told this day I could not become an engraver because of my age. I will become a master before two more years come to pass. I will teach, I will have my dreams of a home and loves become true. I know this in my heart.

Today I had my vision checked, new glasses are required, must sell all the rest of my tools to survive these difficult times. Money enough for one more week of hotel rent. Eating well, gaining back my weight. Sleeping well, but still lonely and after school cold and bored. Washing my clothes in the bathtub, drawing sketches to pay for meals, boots still hurting my feet, But where there is a will, there is a way. The hotel owner is a nice and kind concerned person; I explained to him that at the rate my money is going I will soon run out of funds. He has moved me out of my second floor room and up into the attic, I can sleep here for no charge. I have gratefully made the move even though the shower is but a drizzle of very cold water.

Although he was kind and concerned, the innkeeper wasn't about to give away the keys to the castle, I had to be in the room by 11 p.m. when he would roll down the iron curtains and lock the place up for the night. The family that owned the Albergo Gardone was very typical Italian. Clean, well dressed, well nourished with a cheerful disposition toward life and labor. Their sense of family was something I could not comprehend; I had spent 42 years with selfish, mean-spirited, cruel, unloving people. Suddenly I was among people who loved passionately, openly and unselfishly.

I felt now that I had really died and Italy was a place for me to be reborn. I felt like an intruder. I was so different. I had worked at so many various types of employment; I had no sense of family, and had so very little happiness in my many affairs with women that I was considering an alternate sexual lifestyle. I believed that women were kin to widow spiders, spinning their tender webs. I thought of myself as a wolf that had been wounded, once by cupid's arrow when I was young then a second time by a beautiful trapper with red hair.

January 24th, 1982

Dear Universal Mind,

Last night I had a dream. I was running, laughing, holding hands with someone, a woman, there were children in the room, boys and girls, black, white and yellow, I was their teacher and they were waiting for me to arrive.

They were also happy and smiling. Then I awoke here in this cold lonely attic, the dream only a pleasant memory, it was 6 a.m. and I cried. I cried because the dream was over. Never had I felt as happy as I did in that dream. Please, let that dream become reality.

That same evening after the dream, I entered the Albergo bar after school. The owner, Pietro Dominici was at his usual place behind the bar dispensing grappa, whiskey and coffee. He greeted me with a big smile. I think he was proud to have me as his guest, after all, the whole town of Gardone knew of the Americano who had entered Giovanelli's school of engraving.

"Come eat something," he would say.

"No, Signore, you give me work and then I will eat."

Soon I was waiting tables and doing the general maintenance around the hotel. Pietro was very concerned about me; he had bought several of my sketches. One evening while I was sitting near the bar drawing, a man entered. There were many "Ciaos," embraces and kisses by the other workers. Pietro introduced me to a strong, bearded man, dressed in brown woolens, hunting jacket, and wearing a green alpine cap. Pietro explained that this man was a great artist and he was willing to give me a job. I was overjoyed; I would have a part time job working for a famous artist. Finally, after more explaining, I understood he was a taxidermist. Taxidermy was right up my alley and a much-needed experience to help with my career. I was to start working for him the following evening after school. After asking several times for directions to this new job, making sure that I understood exactly where the place was, I retired for the night with great expectations for the next day.

School was going well, or at least better. I sold the vise that I had dragged halfway around the world to my teacher Renato and bought a new pair of eyeglasses. I had learned to speak and understand some Italian, enough to survive. For the first two weeks of school, I ate no lunch because I did not understand that the school had its own cafeteria with good lunches for workers and students.

On this momentous day, a very wealthy, important looking man was touring the school; he was Italian but spoke perfect English. Signor Giovanelli brought him over to my workstation to look at the practice plate I was engraving. After a few brief questions, the man explained about the cafeteria, I could eat there for $2 a meal. I told him that I had no money extra for lunch. To that, the man replied that he, meaning Signor Giovanelli, would like me to eat as his guest.

Those lunches not only gave me the nourishment needed but introduced me to the flavors of Northern Italian cooking. Signor Giovanelli's school provided me with food, the food needed to survive. At lunch each day, I would try to be the last served. Then would delay my departure until all of the students, workers, and staff finished, leaving the cafeteria empty. I would then go around to their plates, stuffing the left over scraps into my jacket pockets for that night's dinner.

I was expecting this newfound job with the taxidermist would provide some much-needed lira. That afternoon when school let out I accepted a ride down the mountain into the town of Gardone with another of the teachers, Giulio Timpini; Giulio was the master engraver for Beretta. He had started engraving at the age of 11 and was at my age when we first met at school. Signor Timpini would drive up to the school every three or four days to spend time with each student. He was a genius with a hammer and a chisel.

Students had a practice plate to do their special work. We could work on those plates Saturday afternoons. Signor Timpini would spend time with us, showing us mistakes, and giving instructions on the many techniques that are part of an engravers varied skills. He instructed us in the art of gold inlay and gold overlay. He showed us the techniques for coin sculpture, under his guidance I learned to cut script, inlay lettering, layout, design, everything. Under Signor Timpini's gentle guidance, my work took great steps forward.

Thanking Giulio, I got out of his car and walked across Via Bernardelli to the taxidermist's shop. Its display windows showed the maestro's skills, mounted wild boar, ibex, doves, wild turkeys, chipmunks, and lions, all sorts of animals mounted and preserved for the contemplation of their killers. For me, a learning artist, I could think of no better place to study wildlife. I entered the shop and found the maestro at work preparing a bull's head for mounting. It looked fascinating with its long tattered ears, eyes black as coal and sneering expression. I could almost sense the rage or imagine a toreador impaled on the tip of one of its black horns, for a brief second I thought about taxidermy for a career. The maestro was a man of few words. It was cold outside but the shop was very warm. I took my coat and cap then hung them on the rack by the door. We shook hands and he led me into another room.

Hanging from the cement ceiling by a rusting meat hook was the severed head of a wild boar. The smell of it was so strong I could hardly control my stomach. I swallowed and settled down.

"I can do this," I thought to myself.

The maestro picked up a sharp knife and began cutting the flesh away from the skin, indicating to me to take the knife and begin. He handed the sharpening stone and the knife to me then pointed to the dead boar's staring eyes, showing me to be careful in cutting those lifeless orbs out, along with lips, ears, and snout. I had no problems dressing out the head, I was a country boy, but oh man, the smell.

I would cut a bit of flesh away, gag, recover, and then do it again. Three hours later the naked skull of putrid flesh was hanging from the hook. The maestro picked up the skin, looked it over and found the work satisfactory, paid me 20.000 lira then pointed at the frozen, bloated body of a fox he had removed from the freezer. He indicated that it would be ready for me the following evening.

The next day at school I could not concentrate. I kept thinking about that defrosting fox waiting at the taxidermist's shop. Lunchtime came. I could not eat. The cursed boots had rubbed my little toe so raw that it had become infected.

That night I explained that I could not cut the fox. Did the maestro have other work? Perhaps I could build the frames for his masterpieces. I sold him my wood carving chisels. They were the last of the tools that I had made. I have always had a passion for hand tools. Those woodworking chisels were my pride. I was very saddened by the necessary sale.

February 20th, 1982

Today I almost gave up, thinking too much about home, and happiness. Sometimes I wonder if I am sane. It would be so easy to quit, get a good job and work for money. To put my brain in neutral, stop thinking, join the great society of the complacent herds. However, when I look and see how others live or exist, I cannot bring myself to join them—at least not at that level. I will never again have a negative thought about my life and each and every day I will shoulder with good will any challenge I have to face with a glad heart and a positive outlook, that way I know I shall succeed at becoming a good artist and a human who can enjoy your blessings.

It was at the end of March that I received a letter from my mother. I found the never mailed answer tucked between the pages of my journal while reviewing these writings

Dear Mother

It was nice to receive your letter. I am trying to enjoy my stay here but it is a little difficult due to the language barrier. I am rapidly learning basic words in Italian, enough to get by. I plan to stay as long as it is possible for me to survive here. I hope that I will be finished by the end of September. I would like to be back in the States for fall. I then intend to find a job as an engraver or as a teacher.

You asked who and what I am. I wish I could tell you exactly but I really do not know. I guess I am an artist, but I am only a mediocre artist. I guess I am a forty-three year old man still trying to find someone to share my life with, that I may grow old and die peacefully.

I feel as though I will accomplish much with the rest of my life now that I live it for me and do as my mind tells me to do, not as society or family expects me to do.

I am your son, of that we are both sure but other than that I am nothing more, nor less than I am. I hope you understand what I am trying to say. I enjoy being me. I do not ever want to be 9-5, one job, day after day. How boring and dull life would be for me. I wish sometimes that I could conform to a life that is considered normal. However, I am darn glad that I don't. Just think! My life is about half over and already I have done and seen more than most people ever dream of doing and I still have half left.

I grant you that I do not have a home or money in the bank but I can always obtain that when it is time. When I am finished here, I should be the most knowledgeable gunsmith in the States, not that I want to be a gunsmith again, a teacher perhaps.

And in another five years, I should be the best engraver in the States. Then I can work at being a great artist until I am old enough to die. When I am old and my body is worn out, I think I will just be very content with my life and myself. I hope that explains who I am.

How am I? Fine! I go to school six days a week, 8:30 am–6 pm. I wash dishes for my supper and have enough rent paid for the next 20 days, and then it will be spring! If it is necessary, I can sleep outside somewhere. School is wonderful! I have some of the finest teachers in the world for both engraving and design.

I have spent many cold nights and quite a few hungry mornings and now weigh about 160 pounds but I am holding my own. I have always been able to take care of myself. Yes, I did get my name changed. Love your son.

Chapter nine

"A REAL LOVE"

One day an engraver named Mimo asked me if I would like to meet a woman who spoke English.

"She's not married and she's very intelligent."

After I said that I would like to meet her, he promised to come by my hotel at 8 p.m. on Thursday. At 8 p.m. I was dressed in clean jeans, maroon turtleneck, and freshly laundered jacket, bathed, shaved, and wearing the recently polished Justin boots. I was ready to turn on that artist charm.

In the short time I had been in Gardone, I had started flirtations with three women: a buxom barmaid, a sexy secretary at the school, and the last a seventeen-year-old College girl who spoke a bit of English. None of them took the attention seriously.

Mimo arrived in his Alfa Romero; he was meticulously dressed, looking more or less like a short Cary Grant. He had been engraving for twelve years and it was against him that I mentally competed at school. My goal was to become a better engraver than Mimo.

He took my continuous examinations of his work with a magnifying lens as a compliment. I would study the cuts made by his chisel, looking for mistakes or rough cuts. I would memorize his work, go to my vise, and practice the cuts he made trying to duplicate them. One day I had just finished cutting a very small scroll about the size of my little fingernail. Every cut was perfect. The spirals within the scroll were so smooth and well cut that I could not resist taking the plate out of the vise. I took it over to Mimo for him to examine. Handing him the loupe, I offered the plate for his examination. After studying the work, he took the plate, put it in his vise, and proceeded to cut a perfect scroll half the size of the one I had finished. He handed the plate back to me and offered me his loupe. I looked through the ten-power lens; every cut he had made was perfect, nothing else needed said; Mimo had put me in my place.

The place Mimo was taking me that night was a pizzeria called The Corral, and was the owner's imaginative creation of a western bar. Mimo parked down the street in the first empty space he could find, locked the car, and then led the way to the entrance of the pizzeria. I walked behind, trying to control the limp of my right foot. Man, I sure looked good in those stolen boots. Mimo opened the door and I followed him into the bar. Bang! I was suddenly in some western bar! Paintings of mustangs racing across the prairie covered one wall. There were long plank tables and chairs and a neon jukebox from the fifties occupied center stage, the air was laden with the aroma of expensive perfume and cigarette smoke. The people at the tables were all eating, drinking, laughing, and having a great time.

"Hey everybody, here is the guy I was telling you about. He's here to learn how to engrave, but he's too old and I think he's crazy." That was his introduction.

I was shocked to find out what he had said several years later. The whole bar went dead quiet. Everyone there was dressed equally as well as Mimo, beautiful women, handsome men, all in their twenties and early thirties. I think I was older than the bar owner. At one of the tables sat five beautiful women. They made space at the table for me. I took the seat opposite from a lovely golden haired, blue-eyed woman, who had the complexion of polished alabaster and her companion with luxurious black hair and the most beautiful dark brown eyes I had ever seen: Fiorella and Franca.

"Hello," she said. "My name is Franca."

It was so good to hear someone speaking English. I had so much bottled up inside and no one to express myself to. I shook her hand and sat down. Franca's first question took me by surprise.

"Do you have identification?" she asked.

"Yes," I had a passport and answered by digging it out of my jeans pocket and handing it to her. We talked for only a few minutes but during that time, I studied her carefully. She was elegantly dressed in a dark brown silk frock decorated in yellow and orange flowers. She wore a simple gold chain around her finely arched neck, matching earrings hung from her delicate earlobes. Tossed carelessly over the back of her chair was a luxurious beaver coat.

"Definitely a city girl," I smiled …

I had received a letter from Marshal Williams, the Virginia lawyer, wishing me success and saying how much he admired the determination it took to learn engraving Enclosed in the letter was a ten-dollar bill. The letter ended by saying,

"Have a pizza or something on me. Your friend, Marshall."

I offered to buy Franca and her friend Fiorella a beer and ordered one for Mimo and me.

"Thank you," Franca replied politely. "I'm leaving early tomorrow morning for the Canary Islands for two weeks and then I shall be going on to Dubai, and after that to Hong Kong. I will be back in about two month's time. It was nice to meet you; perhaps we shall meet again, Goodnight." And with that, Franca and her good friend Fiorella left.

"Put her out of your mind, pal," that voice said to me, "She's definitely way out of your league."

Mimo was having a good time with his friends so I retired off to the corner, finished the beer, listened to music for a while, and then went back to the hotel that was just a short distance away. The pain in my foot was too intense to ignore any longer.

From my journal:
Last night, nightmares again, not much progress in my engraving. Today will be a better day. The boots have become a real problem for me but I have no alternative. Even a country boy finds it difficult to walk barefoot in cold and snow.

One spring evening after school I was hobbling along the street headed towards the hotel when a car pulled up alongside. I paid no attention to it or its driver. Suddenly a feminine voice says to me,

"Hey honey, where are you going?"

I thought, "Who in the hell could be calling me honey?"

I looked up to see Franca in her little white Fiat Panda. She pulled over to the curb. I recognized her but didn't recall her name.

"Hey, nice to see you, when did you come back?" I asked.

Instead of answering my question, she asked me, "Why are you walking so funny?

I answered, "These boots hurt my feet."

"Why are you wearing them if they hurt your feet?"

"Lady, it's the only pair I have to wear."

"Oh, I see," she answered, then said "Would you like to go somewhere with me this Saturday afternoon?"

"Sure, I'd like that," I answered.

"I'll pick you up in front of the hotel at four."

Smiling, she put the car in gear and roared off up the hill, leaving me standing there with mouth agape in wonderment.

Saturday at 4 o'clock, I was dressed and waiting out in front of the hotel. Just as the church bells began to ring the hour, Franca flew into the square. The Fiat squeaked to a stop. I was truly surprised. The woman had shown up on time. I was impressed. I walked over to the car as she rolled down the window. "Get in," she said. "I want to take you somewhere."

I barely seated myself when we were off with a squeak and a lurch. Franca went chatting on about my school and how was I doing. She seemed oblivious to the traffic, pedestrians, bicycles, and the very narrow and winding streets. She kept that beautiful foot of hers pressing on the accelerator while she continued chatting away. I was holding on, expecting a head-on collision any second. I was sure she was going to kill someone. I kept thinking, "I made it all the way to Italy, and this crazy woman is going to kill me in her car. This is not funny, God. Not funny at all."

Finally, to my relief she stopped the car. I had no clue where I was. I had been so very busy watching the traffic, expecting a crash, that I had lost my direction. I know we were several miles from the hotel. I was seriously considering walking back.

"Come into the house," Franca said.

We got out and walked into someone's home. I expected to meet a relative or a friend. "Sit down in that chair please," Franca, said to me. "I'll be right back."

She disappeared through the curtains of a doorway, soon reappearing with a man carrying boxes of tennis shoes.

"Now please take those boots off."

I was flustered. "What?" I asked.

"Please take those boots off. I want you to try on these tennis shoes."

"Me, take off these boots? No ma'am, I'm not going to do that."

"I want to buy these shoes for you," she insisted.

"No ma'am, I don't take charity."

"I want to buy them for you as a present," Franca insisted. Presents I could handle, I began pulling off the boots. My sock was an embarrassment. It was bloody and smelled not that nice. She insisted that I put on new socks before trying on the shoes. With much professionalism, the clerk measured my feet, selected a pair of white tennis shoes, and slipped them on.

"Stand up and walk around," said Franca. Numbly I followed her instructions.

"Walk over here. Walk over there. Turn around. Are they comfortable?" Comfortable was not an apt description. My feet had left my body and ascended into heaven.

March 26, 1982
Today my engraving took a large step forward. I received many encouraging words
from some of the other engravers. I am in fine and good spirits. Thank you for loving
me.

Although I was grateful for the tennis shoes, I really had no intention of becoming involved with Signorina Franca Facchetti. She was pert, sexy, independent, and free spirited. Exactly what I was looking for in a mate, but neither of us was looking for permanency. I considered the gift of those shoes kind-hearted, but I was deep into my engraving career and that took all priorities.

Franca lived about three blocks from the Piazza Gardone and the hotel .We would occasionally meet, she returning from work and I from school. I clearly recall our first so-called date. She took me for pizza, ribs, and wine at a restaurant called Oasis. One of her several ex-boyfriends owned it. Each meeting between us would become a little more sexual than the last, holding hands, laughing, looking into one another's eyes. The end of each encounter would find me alone, in the attic, lying naked on the cot, masturbating. Some old habits never die, they say.

I may not have been in love but I was certainly in lust. One very wet and cold evening the mountain town of Gardone shone white with soft falling drizzle of snow. Franca and I had been invited to a mutual friend's house for dinner. Our friend's names were Anna and her husband Evaristo; He had lived in Morocco, Amsterdam and various other places. He spoke some English, loved to drink, shoot pool, and play soccer. He wore his hair in a long ponytail. Evaristo and I would shoot pool together before I had even met Franca. They lived in the adjacent apartment building. Getting to know Franca, I learned that she had lived in that very same apartment for the better part of her life. She, her two sisters, her mother and gunsmith father had shared the small four-room apartment for twenty-six years. She had a fine job, traveled all over the world first class, had her own car and recently acquired in the same building an apartment of her own, she spoke three other languages and had no addictive habits.

She, like me, had no interest in a permanent relationship. That was about the only thing we had in common. I was so unstable, so naked in my emotions. I was still sleeping half-awake. I was having nightmares and had not slept with a woman in months.

After dinner, Franca decided to walk with me back to the Albergo Gardone hotel. We walked slowly down the street slippery with the new-fallen snow. Franca was bundled up in her fur coat, dressed in a comfortable pair of warm boots and a brown wool skirt. She held tightly to my arm as we slipped and slid our way over the wet cobblestones down to the hotel. I can still visualize her standing in the swirl of sparkling snowflakes, the dim lighting from the shops making the setting postcard perfect. We stopped at the iron gate of the hotel.

"Well," she said squeezing my arm. "Goodnight." She released my arm and started to turn around.

"You're not getting away that easily," I said.

Arms around her waist I pulled her close to me and kissed her fully on those beautiful lips. I held her gently, our lips pressed together, tasting each other until I felt the resistance leave her body.

"Goodnight," I replied, released her, and then entered the hotel.

On the following Saturday, we went out for dinner with more friends and the evening passed quickly. After walking Franca to her apartment, I turned downhill to the hotel. When I got there, the shutters were down and the huge iron gates to the courtyard, locked. I hurried back up the hill to Franca's apartment. I got to the gate and rang the buzzer. In a moment, Franca appeared at the door. I explained my circumstances. The gate clicked open.

April 1982: Sunday

Today I was supposed to paint the large iron gates at the rear of the hotel but it was raining. I'm glad of that for I feel tired and I'm going to stay in bed all day. I now have $40 left but my rent is secure for another month, as is my food. Therefore, I am very rich. I have met a wonderful person here in Gardone. Her name is Franca and she seems nice. She is good to me and has asked nothing from me, for the first time in my life, I feel at peace with myself.

"Watch yourself, Joseph, you're falling in love. No, I will not let that happen to me again. It is much too painful. How can I ever trust a woman again?"

All these thoughts were going around in my head while walking up the winding mountain road to school the following day.

"I'll enjoy the affection but I'm not going to leave my heart unguarded. She is nice though." I enjoyed the fresh early morning air, the new tennis shoes giving wings to my heels

I do not know exactly what happens when someone enters into a relationship. Perhaps you smile more, walk differently, or glow. It did not take long for my art teacher to notice. The whole school knew the American had met someone. In fact, the whole town knew.

Signor Campanelli, my art teacher, was my closest friend at school. We could communicate by drawing.

"A woman?" he asked.

I nodded my head. He smiled and patted my shoulder.

Signor Giovanelli's youngest daughter Maria was about to celebrate her seventeenth birthday. A party was going to be held at the villa for all the students, and we could bring a guest. I decided to ask Franca to accompany me. That night after school, I walked up to her apartment and rang the gate bell. Suddenly two heads appeared over the third story balcony, Franca and her younger sister Giuliana. They looked down and started laughing. Franca had just noticed that I was quite bald.

"Would you like to go to the school Thursday night with me? One of the students is having her birthday party." I asked.

"What time is the party?" The giggling Franca replied.

"7 p.m."

"I'll pick you up at the hotel," the still-smiling Franca whispered then disappeared behind the balcony doors.

Thursday evening, I had just taken an icy shower and was naked except for a towel; I hurried back to the room to towel off and dress for the party, my skin covered with goose bumps from the cold. I entered the room, shut the opaque glass door, stripped off the towel, and started drying my body. Suddenly I heard Franca's voice from the other side of the closed door.

"Are you in there, Joseph? It's me ..."

She is twenty minutes early. I have never known a woman to be early in my entire life.

"Just a minute," I called out while grabbing the towel and re-wrapping my body just as the door opened.

I could not stop myself from staring. She was so beautiful.

In her arms, she was carrying a large bouquet of flowers composed of gladiolas, ferns and a flower I had never seen before called a "bird of paradise." Not knowing what to do I just stood there open-mouthed, hanging onto the towel.

"You can't go to Maria's birthday party without bringing her a present," Franca said. "I brought these for you to give her"

Bang! I fell in love with her at that very moment. I knew she was created for me. It was not long after that she invited me to live with her in her apartment. She has been my constant friend, confidant, and advisor since that day.

June 20th, 1982

Thank you for answering my prayers. I am happy. Happier than I've ever been in my entire life, Franca is wonderful, full of life, honest, loving, caring, and intelligent. Everything I have dreamt of. I promise you I will love and cherish her until I die ... That I will always be honest and truthful, that I will live my life in such a manner that you shall be proud of me.

I know that you exist and that you care for your creations provided they care for themselves.

Dear Universal Mind,
Please grant us these three wishes:
That we will always remain deeply in love
That we will always have good health
That we will have enough wealth to enjoy the world you created.

Joseph and Franca

Chapter ten

"LOVING AND LEAVING ITALY"

Gone with my loneliness were also the last obstacles at school. Soon I was learning the more advanced techniques of engraving: precious metal inlay, relief, sculpting, and the art of printmaking were also part of my studies. I was impatient to cut my own designs. Like any other artist, I wanted the work to be my own, to be original. Maestro Sanzgoni would not allow me that freedom.

"If you want to be a good engraver, you must copy the other engraver's works," he kept reminding me

"Here," he would say pointing to a floor plate of a model 70 Winchester rifle. "This is good engraving. You copy this."

Model 70, floor plate

The months at school flew by. My time with Franca and her gentle ways started the healing process. Franca would always pay for our trips to restaurants, weekends in Florence, days on Lago d'Iseo, a trip to Bolzano, Rimini. Every time we would go somewhere, I would protest that she was spending too much money.

"I'll pay now. You can pay later. She would say. You cannot worry about money. You must concentrate on your engraving."

My love for Italy, its people, its food and culture grew with every day that passed.

In August after the summer holidays, I returned to school and started engraving my own plates. The plate I had been working on at school was a very thick block of steel. When one side was full of practice, engraving the plate was taken to the machine shop where it was milled down of the work and the apprentice engraver would start over. I knew that one day I would be leaving school and I needed to have a portfolio of my work. I asked my Maestro if he could get some stainless steel plates for me to engrave on.

The day of departure from Giovanelli's Bottega d'Incisione came sooner than I wanted. Franca and I were really starting to discover one another. We would hike in the hills of Gardone, laughing and holding hands like children. She was carrying the weight and I was worry free. One morning at the start of school, Cesare Giovanelli sent for me and informed me that school was over. I shook my head not understanding. School was supposed to take three years. I loved school; I did not want it to end. His interpreter explained to me that I had been an exceptional student and had learned all there was and that it was now time to return to the United States where my work could be my teacher.

From my journal:
Have decided to leave Italy about September 15. But before leaving I will cut six more practice plates and make each one better than the last and when the last one is done it will be some of the finest engraving seen in a long time.

The realization that I must soon return to the United States carried with it a mixed bag of emotions and decisions. And Franca was in the middle of it.

I was very much in love with her. I was sure she was in love with me. She referred to our first meeting as me being a naked man. I had no hidden agenda. I thought of her as a woman who was honest. If she could love me at the lowest point of my engraving career, she would not destroy me once I had become successful. I knew also that getting started was not going to be easy. I had no passage back to the United States. I was planning to return by working out passage aboard a freighter or if that failed, throwing myself on the mercy of the U.S. embassy. I agonized over what to tell her. She had such a beautiful life when she met me. I did not want her to end up as wreckage in my life. I had all I could stand of those types of emotional traumas. I had no problems in trying to take care of myself. However, Signorina Franca Facchetti was another matter.

First, I decided it was best to leave her a note. I would disappear like a thief in the night, it would be best. She would forget about me in a short while, I could not let her be hurt. Finally, I decided to tell her that school was over and I would soon be returning to the United States. I was very sure of the skills I had learned; I knew I was a good engraver, having studied enough of the other engravers works to know good work from bad and in 1982, there were several engravers making very good livings in the United States turning out mediocre work. I had decided that on my return to try the gun manufacturers on the East Coast for employment.

During my studies at Giovanelli's I had met some of the important people of the firearms industry: several executives from Winchester, the famous firearms authority Larry Wilson, along with several people from Beretta USA. I was sure to find work. It was more a question of how long it would take and as we all learn, time is money.

A month before my departure I talked to Franca, explaining how I felt about her, the trip back, and my insecurities. The ever-practical Franca's answer was,

"I've always wanted to visit the United States. I will sell my car to my sister, and give notice at my job. I have wanted to quit for some time now and this is a good time to do it. I will sublet the apartment to my friend Fiorella and her lover Carlo, and then I will go with you." From my journal:

September 1st, 1982,

Schooling is almost complete. September 15th, Franca and I will be leaving Gardone. To the best of my knowledge, I will be going to work for Winchester on my return.

As the departure date drew nearer, I continued to work on my portfolio. I had no photos of things I had engraved. Actually, I had engraved two cheap handguns in my entire professional career and would never admit to anyone that the work was mine.

From my journal:

Today I made my first prints from my engraving. Now I am positive that I can do it. There are many mistakes and still a long way to go to become a great artist engraver, but I can do it.

Dear Universal Mind,

Thank you for helping me with all your blessings. They have been many. Many times when I felt so sad and alone and misunderstood, if you had not been my strength, I would have given up. Whatever life has in store, I will always remain your servant.

The engravers at Giovanelli were all considerably younger. Yet, all had been engraving for several years and most of them had taken the time to engrave a plate in the banknote style or what the Italians call Bolino, a method of engraving in which the steel plate is covered with microscopic dots made by a handheld burin. The work is slow and very tedious but the results are so exquisite, the work, very impressionistic. I had made friends with all of them. Each engraver gave me a print off a plate they had engraved as a going away gift. I had no way of thanking them so I made my last plate at school a print plate done with a portrait of a setter dog surrounded by arabesque scroll. The plate took three weeks to cut.

I can still feel the excitement of that day, my last day of school. I carefully inked the plate and wiped it clean of the surface ink, positioned the plate in the center of the intaglio press's heavy steel base, carefully took a dampened sheet of French rag paper and laid it on top of the plate. Then placed the layers of thick wool felt on top of that single sheet of paper. When all was ready, I ran the whole sandwich of plate, ink, paper, and felt, under the steel rollers of the huge iron press. Tons of pressure forced the paper into each and every cut made on that two inch square piece of polished steel, picking up the ink that remained in those thousands of pinpricks, how my heart raced with pride and joy when the felt was removed, exposing the paper. The print was to determine my future. Was I truly going to be a great engraver?

Signor Giovanelli lifted the print from the plate. Holding my first creative effort under his loupe, he began to examine the print. Every cut stood out clear and sharp. The work itself had beauty and sensitivity in its rendering. He smiled and then said he would be pleased to write for me a letter of introduction.

Portrait of a setter

I printed about a dozen copies of that plate and gave them to the other engravers and one to Signor Giovanelli as well. To Mario Abbiatico I also gave a print. His words to me on that very day were.

"Joseph, when I first saw the work you had done in the United States, I thought you were hopeless. Then after I found out how you had arrived here, I thought you were crazy, but now that I know you, I think you have the largest pair of balls of any man I have ever met. You have the three things that it takes to make a great engraver: heart, passion, and strong hands. God bless you and Franca on your return to the United States."

We shook hands and embraced. I felt that familiar lump in my throat. I smiled and walked away with an autographed copy of the book that had brought me to Italy, held proudly in my hands.

Like every awaited moment in life, the time for our departure finally arrived. Franca had many friends in Italy, the last few days were spent eating out, drinking toasts, hugging, kissing, and some weeping on the part of Franca's mother. Maria Teresa, Franca's older sister, who was sure I was an escaped felon, kept insisting that this was a big mistake. Her boss was telling her the same thing but Franca with her unusual courage and determination decided to go.

Chapter eleven

"SELF RESPECT"

September 17th, 1982 found us in New Haven, Connecticut. The plane trip back to the States was nothing like the trip over. I was no longer a sad desperate man. I was a different person totally. My biggest personal concern was Franca.

We arrived in New Haven in a rented car then found a clean and inexpensive motel for the night. That night we went out to a Chinese restaurant for our first meal together in the United States.

Early next morning I left Franca at the motel and arrived at the corporate offices of U.S. Repeating Arms Company with my portfolio of engraved plates. I explained to the receptionist who I was and what I wanted. She in turn brought me to the personnel director's office. After looking at my work, he contacted the head of the Winchester custom shop, a man named Pardee, who looked at my work and then contacted his boss Mr. Carl Hummel. It was about two hours later that I was offered a job.

"Yes, we need an engraver. You have a job with us," Carl said.

"What is the salary?" I asked.

I have forgotten the exact amount it was, around $9 or so. I was disappointed. I thought back to school and the bloody boots. I decided to bluff.

"I'm sorry," I said. "I'm not interested. I already have an appointment with a company in California. I just stopped to see if you were interested in me."

What did I expect to receive as compensation for my work, the personal director wanted to know. I held my breath for a moment and then asked for $30,000 per year. They asked me leave the meeting. Richard Pelton, president and CEO of U.S. Repeating Arms Company came into the conference room about that time and shook hands with me. After a careful study of my portfolio, he explained employment at that salary would have to be a corporate decision. I wanted to know when I could have an answer. After a brief meeting, they told me that the decision would take a week. A week of meals and motels would quickly eat up all of Franca's money. I bluffed again.

"I'm sorry. I cannot stay that long. I have to be in California in a few days."
The truth was there were no appointments with anyone. If I lost this gamble, I
could lose it all. I had gone too far to back down.

"Where are you staying?" President Pelton asked.

Not wanting to say I was staying at a motel 2 ½, answered, "In a small motel
near town."

"Would you consider postponing your trip to California until we can make a
decision if Winchester puts you up in the Park Plaza Hotel? Of course we'll pick
up all the expenses." I explained that I had a friend with me. "Not a problem," he
told me. I do not think I have ever had a bigger smile on my face.

"Yes sir," I answered, shook hands all around and went back to get Franca and
tell her the greatest news. When we had returned the car, we checked into the
hotel laughing and dancing in the lobby as though we were at a carnival. When
the desk clerk said "Welcome to the Park Plaza Mr. Joseph, have a wonderful
stay" Franca whispered, "I'm so glad I met you Amore."

From my journal:
September 18th, 1982 Hartford, Connecticut
Since arriving here, Franca and I have been guests of U.S. Repeating Arms Com-
pany. We are staying in the nicest hotel room I have ever been in, in my life. The room
cost about $145 per day and my bill here for at least four days is going to be close to
$600—more money than I have earned in the last year.

A few days later, the personnel director came to the hotel with an employment
contract for me to look over. Winchester had met my salary demand, made me a
part of the company's executive staff, in charge of the engraving department, and
had given me the title of Master Engraver. In addition to all of this, there was
$1000 check to help us settle in. After, the excitement that I felt over those last
few days passed, the cold realization that I had never engraved an actual rifle
replaced it. I was cocky, proud of myself, and quickly developed a bit of an attitude.

I returned to the Company to deliver the signed contract to Mr. Hummel,
who gave me complete tour of the factory, and introduced me to all the employees of the custom shop. To my surprise there was a woman working in the
engraving room her name was Pauline Murray. Obviously, she was not at all
happy with the idea of having a new boss. I looked at the work she was doing and
immediately thought I would be able to help her improve her skills. Then I met
Bruno Pardee, head of the custom shop, who also was not thrilled with the fact

that I was receiving a salary higher than his, and that I worked directly for Carl Hummel. Not that I really cared, I was too excited and proud of my accomplishments to even consider the pettiness and pitfalls of working in a unionized company,

My presence in the long, four-story, brick building that housed the custom shop for the famous Winchester 21 shotguns was quickly noted. Soon the entire floor knew everything about me, especially my salary. This caused some friction between me and several other employees who had worked their way up through the rank and file to end up working at the most prestigious part of the Winchester Gun Company.

The custom shop was where the wealthy would spend their money. At the time of my employment, a model 21-shotgun base price was $10,000. The same weapon engraved with gold inlay sold for $25,000. The company expected the engraver to finish the work in approximately 130 hours.

I had a meeting with Carl Hummel shortly after my arrival. Carl was a very kind man with a sharp business sense. He outlined for me his idea. He wanted to have ready for exhibition at the Dallas Shot Show at least three engraved rifles and one shotgun.

The date of that exhibition was January 11, exactly one year since I had gotten on the plane headed for Italy. I was a very proud and happy man. Franca and I had grown closer together. The upcoming exhibition was consuming me. Thousands of people would see my engraving work at the biggest sporting goods show in the United States. How so very different things were now. The Company decided I would do engraving exhibitions for the public during the three-day show. Everybody was going to be there. Many of my Italian friends, fellow engravers from Gardone, Maestro's Renato and Giulio, Signor Giovanelli, engravers from Colt, the most famous engravers in the world would be there and I was part of it.

I was not one of the wannabes in the massive lines of people, peeking and peering. No, sir, I was one of the top dogs. How can I ever forget the trembling of my excited hands, people taking photos, asking for autographs, the flashing cameras? I will always remember how good it felt to wear a new white shirt, Italian loafers and silk tie, gifts from Franca's sister. I had gray wool slacks and a sports coat with a nametag pinned neatly across the right hand breast pocket: Joseph, Master Engraver, U.S. Repeating Arms Company. I still have that tag as a memento.

Model.94/22 rifle, my first design

The plane trip to Dallas was also in sharp contrast to a year earlier. U.S. Repeating Arms took care of shipping vise, tools, and personal luggage directly the Dallas Hilton. Carl's secretary gave me my tickets and expense account vouchers. I was ready for my first public debut. The rifles I had engraved for the show consisted of one Model 94/22, the first real gun engraving I ever did.

I labored over the design and made every cut in that steel with heart in my mouth. I could ruin the entire work with one slip of the chisel. It took forty hours to design the weapon and then engrave it. It sold the first day of the show for $6,500.

Model 94 rifle, factory design

The second rifle I engraved was a Model 94 carbine. I engraved it in the common factory style.

It sold also on the first day to the curator of the Winchester firearms museum located in Cody Wyoming. All four pieces of my work sold that weekend in Dallas.

My head was dizzy with pride; people were stopping to admire the labor that I had invested in the model 94 rifle engraved for the show. It was of my own design and the training received in Italy had great influence over the effect.

Model 94 Winchester, my design

January 11ᵗʰ, 1982

In Dallas, fame came to me with a roar. It left my head spinning, hands shaking, palms sweating. It gave me a look at a new world of restaurants without prices on the menu. $10,000 wristwatches, gold chains, and diamond rings. The first thing I did was run to hide. Hide in a greasy spoon with a jukebox, dirty floors, good food, and uncomplicated people. Later, at the hotel, people would look at me but not speak. People who were friendly before were now distant in sort of a silent jealousy. I felt alone, afraid I was going to change into someone that I would not like. I will not change though. Never will I forget my roots or the lessons that I have learned from the school of life.

Tomorrow will be one year since I got on the plane to London. Now it seems like a dream, unreal, impossible. Yet I did it. Despite the hardships and most of all, the doubts and the lack of encouragement from people I met along the way. I do not blame *them, for I must have seemed **out** of my mind for an average person. I can never forget the pain both mental and physical. At this moment I feel drained, completely used up, no energy left. Yet I know in a few days that I'll be right back at it, looking for more mountains to climb. I wish I could explain to someone how I feel inside, why I knew, and how I know I will become an artist such as this country has rarely seen, but I can't, I just feel it so within me. I know I will be an old man someday, and when I die, the world will cry for me. However, it will also be a better place.*

At the Shot Show were many private collectors who were interested in having some of my engraving, among them was a man named Merrill Lindsay. He was the curator of another Firearms Museum, the Eli Whitney Museum. He outlined a project that would supply me with 100 Whitney rifles to engrave, about a years work. The project was a year away from production, but Mr. Lindsay was impressed enough to offer me the job of designing the prototype. I returned from Dallas with the future looking its brightest ever, reentering the engraving room of the company with a new excitement.

Model 21 Grand American, U.S. Arms Co.

The company had received an order for a special Winchester, a model 21 shotgun for an investment firm in Canada. They wanted me to do the engraving in the style of "The Grand American." The gold work consisted of sculpted roses and maple leaves.

This meant that all of the lettering had to be inlaid with gold wire; two bands of gold were cut and inlaid into the barrels, the gun frame covered with the finest English scroll and a portrait of a setter inlaid with gold, on the trigger guard. This was to be a most complex piece of work. Having only, a brief amount of time to study the techniques of inlaying gold lettering, I was very nervous and concerned that I might screw the whole thing up. One slip of the chisel could cost $10,000. I recall with clarity standing in front of the vise, chisel in my left hand, and hammer in the right, the polished steel gun frame positioned in the vise. I stood there, arms raised, prepared to make the first cut into the precious metal, cold sweat was dipping from my armpits. Then I thought a silent prayer. "Thank you for giving me this day. Thank you for giving me life, guide me." I would make the first cut.

The problems encountered in engraving are multiple. You have no idea exactly how hard the steel is, Too hard and the delicate point of the razor sharp chisel will break, seriously scratching the work. Too soft and the chisel will sink too deeply impairing the safety factor of the weapon.

There also is the complexity of the design, and the manufacturing of small-hardened bits of steel into the miniature tools that are required to inlay gold. Great care is necessary neither to mar the finely polished surface of the receiver nor to crush it with the jaws of the vise. Over the years I've executed detailed figures, portraits in steel, and in gold inlaid in steel, in a space no larger than my little finger nail. Another factor is of course time. Time is money and when a piece of work was in the vise, I would work at it diligently until it was finished. I could do a good gold portrait brought to its finest detail in two hours after I had been engraving for ten years, but this was the very first one and it was going on a $25,000 shotgun.

With sweat-soaked shirt, I made the first cut into the precious steel. My grip was too firm, the wrist too stiff, and the swing of the hammer was off center, but the chisel point held. I corrected my grip and soon the chisel was cutting smoothly. Now it was only a matter of hitting the end of the chisel perfectly, and for the next 120 hours or so, following the curving, rolling design, I had marked on the polished steel with a .03-millimeter pencil.

I hope this gives you, dear reader, a greater understanding of why such a small number of people have taken up this noble, challenging, and lucrative trade. The money I was earning soon allowed me to rent a car, drive back down to Lynchburg, Virginia, to pay off the check I had written for those blessed Justin boots. I also bought my friend from Maine a new rifle to replace the one I had wrongly sold, and sent it to him with his initial engraved in the floor plate along with an apology and explanation. Joseph was a man of his word and this was to be part of my reputation as a professional engraver.

An engraver's reputation has to be sterling, and Joe LaVarnois's was a long cry from being a trust worthy character. My amazing Franca understood.

"It's OK, Joseph. I understand," she said, when I told her that Red and I were still not divorced. I contacted Red through her mom and quickly received my divorce papers. Red paid for the divorce. I was finally a free man.

Thanksgiving Day, November 24, 1982. In the corner of my living room, complete with drawing table, stools, pens, pencils, warmth and love I sat down to read this journal in its entirety. Every thing has come to me. Every wish I made has been granted. Perhaps not at the moment of asking but they have all been fulfilled. I now have money, friends, respect, and most of all, the woman of my dreams. People find my work beautiful, yet I know it has a long way to go.

Chapter twelve

"OLD DEBTS"

January 1983 was the year of settlements of old debts and a new lifestyle for the man I was, not the man I used to be. I had many unresolved personal problems in the U.S. that needed settling. First, had been the rubber checks, then squaring accounts with Mr. Moran and then ending my previous marriage.

Now I had only two nasty, ugly, sticky affairs to settle. Both of these were with the collections agencies of the federal government. One was about back support to one ex-wife. The other was with the IRS for taxes. I was very worried about the IRS, as I had not paid taxes for many, many, many years. Now that I was a legitimately salaried employee, Joseph had to start paying his income taxes, something that Joe L. had not done for close to twenty years.

It all started when Joe got a part-time job. The job was piecework and paid in cash. I guess it was January of '64. I returned home with my tax statement as prepared by H&R Block. I owed the federal government $25. I didn't have $25 to spare so I put the tax statement in a shoebox where it wouldn't get messed up, lost, torn up by one of the kids, or eaten by our black Labrador. It was January of the next year that I recalled my civic duty. This year H&R Block said I owed penalties and interest plus the $25, plus this year's taxes. This statement also went into the shoebox. It was five or six years later that I stopped going to H&R Block every January. Finally, conscience and fear got the better of me.

I decided to confess to the Internal Revenue Service. Taking the shoebox, I found the way to their offices in downtown Portland Oregon and threw myself upon their mercy.

"How long since you filed taxes?" Mr. Suit and Tie asked.

"Ten or eleven years," I replied.

Shortly after that, Agent #2 has read the Miranda warning, and I am advised of my rights.

"Do you have your tax statements," Suit and Tie wants to know.

"No, sir," I said, handing him the still-clean shoebox containing the H&R forms plus a few other W2 forms I had saved until I gave up on the whole idea of paying taxes. Later, that same day I left the federal building carrying with me a pardon.

All I needed to do was sign the enclosed forms clutched in my sweaty hand, then, send a check for $5,000 made out to the Internal Revenue Service, Ogden Utah.

I put the pardon in the shoebox and forgot about it for another ten years.

Explaining all of this to Franca as best I could. She said,

"I understand Joseph, it's all right. We shall file the taxes, starting now."

I pleaded with her not to. I was sure the FBI would be beating down the door in a matter of days after filing; I looked at our mail with trepidation for weeks. The day came when the official envelope finally arrived; I gave it to Franca saying, "You open it."

After a short silence, she clapped her hands, laughed, and said, "You got a refund check of $1,700. Let's go to dinner tonight!"

I waited until after dinner and wine to open the last basket of snakes that nested in Joe LaVarnois's life. The issues of back support, also the need to return to see my children, and the fact, that I was not going to be one of Winchester's executive staff for much longer. Franca knew how deeply hurt I was over the courts decision to leave my children in the custody of Marcelle. I had told her how much I wanted to be near them, she also knew that I was in arrears with child support. We discussed these things again while having espresso and tiramisu.

"Franca," I asked, "What do you think I should do?"

"We'll face it together," she answered. "I'll find out what to do."

She smiled and said, "It will be fine, leave it to me. I'll find out what needs to be done …"

It took several anxious weeks to get things sorted out. The fact that I only had one name caused most of the delays. There are many times in life when I wish I had not been quite so brash. Then overall, it has turned out to be very interesting. Living with one name has been a lot of fun. Think of it as more of a voyage through unexplored seas.

Artists are not normal people. We do see things differently, in different lights and darks. Where people see buildings, we see trees, birds, flowers, people at their toils, clouds, a blue sky with a hole in the middle of it and a building. Why is it we are different? I have no clue.

I could already see that it would not be possible for me to stay employed. I had been at the company for but a few months and was losing enthusiasm for the corporate life style rapidly. I wanted to create, not copy. I could not visualize myself cutting number three style engraving on Winchester model 94s for the rest of my life and said so to Franca.

"I'm going to quit this job. I want to move to Oregon, teach my sons the trade."

"When do you want to do that?" my love asked.

"In the fall," I said.

"We'll need money," she continued. "I'll start a budget and see if I can find a job to help out."

From my journal:
January 9th, 1983
Welcome home Joseph, I have missed you very much and am glad you are back. Congratulations, please remember you do not owe anything to anyone, not even to me. I just love you. Maybe our love gave you extra strength to go on but that is all. You may be grateful to people like Renato Sanzogni, Fausti, and Giovanelli who have taught you engraving but being grateful does not mean you owe them something. What you have accomplished is a result of your efforts and only God knows how hard you have tried. Yes, there may be somebody you owe something to and it is Joseph, nobody but you. Remember you told me. A poor student does not excel his master. I was a good student. I have learned a great deal from you and now I tell you what you told me: You cannot live your life for somebody else. You may make things worse. Everybody has his own way to go and you might be surprised at how well they can do. You can be kind to them, remember them with affection, but that doesn't mean that you owe them something.

Capito, Love,
Franca

The length of time immigration would allow Franca to stay on her tourist visa was half over. We were both free spirited, independent people and really had no need for a wedding ceremony to bind us to one another but the system of government required it. So it was on February 14th, 1983 Franca and Joseph said their vows in front of the justice of the peace in New Haven, Connecticut. Franca and Joseph had been two tiny atoms of flesh and bone drifting in the word's cosmos, unaware of each other being alive, yet believing that they would one day find each other. Then one day, it happened. Now they stood beside one another, she ready to make a lifetime commitment, I terrified of screwing up for the third time.

Franca looked so very beautiful standing five foot four in high heels, so slender and lithe with full red lips that smiled at me over ivory teeth.

Her eyes held a mischievous smile reflecting from the dark brown irises. Her Mediterranean complexion and healthy black hair framed in a white fox stole, a white silk blouse, and white slacks. I held her delicate hand in mine, looked wordlessly into her eyes, trying to communicate the depth of my love for her. As we stood together waiting for the justice of the peace to arrive, my beautiful bride whispered to me these words: "I have waited 32 years to marry and who am I going to be? Mrs. Nobody." she softly sighed.

The spring and summer of our first year of marriage was almost like a fairytale. In the beginning, a beautiful rich woman falls in love with starving artist. He becomes successful. They marry, return to Italy for a honeymoon etc. etc. However, our life was much deeper and richer than a fairytale. Once decided I wanted my freedom back, I began making plans for our future. There were many things I needed to learn about engraving—technical things, tricks of the trade, so to speak. I could only learn them by returning once more to Italy.

I went to see Carl Hummel in his office. I had just completed the engraving on the Investment Grade Model 21 shotgun and was starting the gold inlay work. Unsure of my work, concerned that should someone shoot the gun the gold might fall out, I wanted to make sure I was doing the inlay work right.

There was a famous Colt engraver, Mr. Alvin White, who also lived in Connecticut; I asked Carl if I could take few days off from work to polish up on inlay techniques.

"What do you mean polish up your techniques? You're supposed to know how already."

Carl reluctantly agreed to give the engraver a call to ask if he would instruct me. The next day he called; the answer from Colt's engraver was yes, he would instruct at the rate of $150 per hour. I asked Carl for a months leave explaining that I could learn everything I needed to know from my Italian friends free. Franca and I could spend our honeymoon in Italy, I could improve my skills, and everyone would be happy. Carl looked at me and said, "We've sold every piece of work you've done and made money on it. You are more than justifying your salary. Take the month off."

We returned to Italy, that month spent there more than compensated for my bruised toes. I went to see Maestro Renato Sanzogni who had opened a small shop of his own. He was, among other things, a printmaker and a master die cutter. He could execute every aspect of the engraver's skill to the highest degree. He was an excellent foundry man producing all sorts of artful objects and, he was my friend. He had become my friend out of respect for my efforts. Renato welcomed me with open arms. I explained to him that I needed to study gold work.

Renato had space in the back of his busy and crowded workshop. The Maestro had space but he did not have an extra engraving vise for me to work on. I went to the local hardware store and bought a new vise. Later I mounted the vise solidly in the back room of Renato's studio, I took a chisel, and engraved across the face of it, "Dear God, Guide me." While doing this, the Maestro came by, and seeing I had engraved something, asked what it meant.

I translated, "mio Dio, guidami."

Then he asked me why?

I explained, "So I would never forget."

Ah! He understood and smiled. I settled down to learn from Maestro Renato the advanced techniques of gold inlay into the steel. This time Renato let me choose the designs. Try to imagine laboring over a space two inch's square five a half days a week, 8-10 hours a day until you have exhausted your patience. Then you rest a bit and begin all over again and that space is made of steel. An engraver goes through this training process.

In many respects, engraving is a form of religion unto itself; the unrelenting attempt to achieve perfection, the never ending struggle to over come impatience, the agony of working so long on hard steel. The thought is constantly in the back of your mind that a slip of the chisel can wreck a thousand hours of labor.

The collecting of engraved weapons is the passion of the privileged few. There are many such weapons sold at the world's finest auction houses, weapons done by other engravers from other periods ... Some far more exquisite than any of the guns I engraved during my career. I can say that easily because it is true. I have spent hundreds of hours studying the masters from the centuries past, to know without a doubt that I never was, nor would become the world's premier engraver. I also knew without a doubt that the time spent working in Renato's shop was priceless.

Almost every engraver I have ever met States-side had an ego problem and carried a bit of a chip on their shoulder. I am included in that group; I have seen professional engravers take on projects beyond their abilities, lose their tempers, throw their tools, and turn to drink or drugs. I found that a puff of cannabis seemed to steady my hands and relax tensions.

It was at Renato's studio that I continued the studies of banknote style engraving, while continuing to refine my gold work.

I bought a black powder dueling pistol; it had very elegant lines and excellent workmanship. It was a perfect canvas on which to display my skills.

I decided that the theme for the replica "La Paige Dueler" was to be nautical and the design should come from the 16th century French gunsmith school; because this was a very delicate and complex gold inlay project, I entitled the work, "The Endeavor." Then started on the lock plate first as it was the easiest piece to engrave as it resembled a practice plate and the space to inlay was about the size of my whole thumb—one inch by two inches.

The first design I chose were gold dolphins leaping from a line of silver. From their mouths, spurted three gold balls and three silver fish leapt from the line of gold to swallow those little gold balls. With Renato's instructions, I prepared the plate for inlay while he returned to his work. It was through Renato that I learned true patience and conquered fears of slips and mistakes.

Renato's shop was no more than his converted living room, his wife worked at the nearby hospital. They had two very playful and demanding girls who would arrive after school let out, shattering the silence of the workshop. Upon their arrival, Renato would attend to their needs, settle them on a small sofa, and instruct them with their schoolwork. When the children would interrupt him with their questions, he would put his tools down, answer their questions, then return to his worktable only to be interrupted every ten minutes. He never lost his patience and he never lost his temper.

As patiently as he answered his children's questions, he answered mine, and the work went slowly forward.

Renato's studio was an engraver's hangout; all of the engravers from the Val Trompia area came to see him as friends and for business. One engraver took a dislike to me and could not understand why I was in Italy.

Signor Roberto Aquelari was Giovanelli's top production engraver. He had more hours in front of his vise than I would ever accumulate in a lifetime. He would arrive at Renato's work shop every evening at twenty minutes past four, joke with Renato a bit and then walk into the back room where I had the vise set up, position himself directly behind my left shoulder, without saying a word and watch me at work.

He would stand there, ten or fifteen minutes, never moving, staring at my hands while I worked. Then he would leave, saying nothing to me, saluting Renato on his way out.

After two or three times of doing this, I became so nervous that my hands would start to tremble as soon as Signor Aquelari would walk into Renato's shop. I am sure that he knew his presence was driving me bonkers. I tried everything to get my nervousness under control: self-hypnotism, mental pep talks, ignore him, he does not exist, don't let him make you nervous. Slowly I started to gain self-control, after about two weeks of this routine, I was able to work without my hands shaking when in his presence.

One day he arrived promptly as usual, stood in his usual place and watched me work. This particular day I was retracing the design with a pencil, carefully checking it over to make sure I had traced every line to perfection.

Suddenly Roberto said, "What are you doing?"

Surprised I almost dropped my pencil.

"I'm correcting the design before I cut it." I answered.

"So you can see your mistakes?" He asked.

"Si, Signor, I can."

"Well, if you can see your mistakes, why are you wasting all your time correcting it with a pencil? Why don't you just take the chisel and make it right. Make you a lot faster." Then he patted my shoulder and left me alone for the rest of my stay

Time always passes so quickly when I am in Italy and when my time with Renato ended, it was with reluctance that Franca and I returned to New Haven and Winchester's custom shops. There I approached my engraving work with a new confidence, my cuts in steel were becoming more fluid, and my designs were developing in their flow and complexity. I was now to the point where I felt confident with all of the skills necessary to set out on my own. I wanted to return to the Pacific Coast somewhere near my children so that I could teach them the engraving trade, and help them to find their way. I wanted to do the things that a father is supposed to do with his sons and daughters: advise, encourage, and love them.

Chapter thirteen

"WESTWARD BOUND"

One evening in our New Haven apartment, I was reading an art magazine when I came across an article about a town in Oregon where there was a developing artist's community. It had several prominent sculptors, potters, and printmakers. A casting foundry with a very good reputation, and was located about 250 miles away from my first wife. This to me was still a little bit too close for comfort but close enough that I could see my children. What made me decide to leave Connecticut and move there was the fact that the name of the town was Joseph.

I was sure that our destiny had to be Joseph, Oregon. Why else would the town be there? I discussed the move with Franca. I had learned that the best way to discuss unpleasant or difficult things is to do so in the most pleasant environment available. This time the place was a small fresh water lake near the town of Westchester, Connecticut.

We had been back from Italy for a couple of months. We were enjoying swimming and picnicking with some friends. On the beach were several children in the 6-10 year old age bracket. They were making castles with the damp sand. I sat down with them and began to sculpt a duck in flight. Soon several children were curiously watching.

One boy, about my youngest son Joe's age asked "Mister Do you know how to make an alligator."

"Sure," I said. "But I need you to help to do it."

Soon we were working together on a huge alligator that was going to swallow the duck. Suddenly the boy looked straight in my eyes and said. "Are you going to be an artist when you grow up?

"I am never going to grow up I replied, "I'm having too much fun."

"Me neither" he grinned and we continued to work side by side.

After finishing the alligator, I said goodbye to him and returned to my child bride and her friends. I told them the story and we all had a good laugh over it. Then Franca with her natural intuition, said,

"You're not happy here, are you?"

I answered that I loved my work but I needed to see my children.

"I can tell my love, I could see it in the way you were playing with that boy."

"I'm sorry Franca, I know I have a good position here and all that but I'm going to help my children. I'm going to teach them."

It was the first of August that I went to see Carl Hummel and gave him six weeks notice.

I said to him, "I know you do not understand, I am proud to have worked here, I know, I should be pleased with my employment. However, if I stay here, all I can ever be is the company engraver. I am an artist and want to see how far in life I go. That is why I must quit."

August 2ⁿᵈ, 1983

Winchester is over for me. I am on my way, returning to my children. September 15 Franca and I will leave here and go to Oregon. Joseph, Oregon is where we will start a new life. There we will earn the trust that you have placed in us. Looking backward I know that I could never have done this without your blessings. And I thank you for the times when you carried me. I ask your forgiveness the times I have failed to conduct myself in accordance with your commandment …, But, I am trying and I know you understand.

The remaining time we had left in our New Haven apartment was short. We were busy making plans for our trip west. This was the third time I had driven coast to coast, so I knew what to expect. Franca on the other hand, had no idea how large the United States of America is.

We needed to buy a car. Every Saturday we would ride our bicycles around New Haven looking for cheap used cars. Having had much experience in buying cheap cars, I had a good idea of what we needed. I found a huge Plymouth station wagon; it had enough cargo space to carry our personal belongings, some furniture, all of the reference books, engraving tools, and engraving vise, and still had plenty of space left over. We called it, "The Ark.

I was busy finishing the projects for the custom shop, and just completed the Investment grade Model 21, and every one was satisfied with it. Meanwhile, engraving in the evenings in our Whitney Avenue apartment.

I had purchased from the company two lever rifles. A model 94/22which Franca drew the design for, and a model 94/Big Bore. That would eventually end up on Christies auction block and began engraving them at home in the evening.

I was planning to use these as display pieces to show potential customers. Both of the weapons were quite beautiful. During my career, I have engraved and sold many beautiful Winchester rifles, each one was a work of love, inspiration, and patience beyond most people's comprehension. I never regretted their sale, or care to repossess them. However, the little 22 rifle that my wife drew a design for, I wish I still had.

Model 94/22 U.S. Repeating Arms, my wife's design

In love, and excited we began selling the modest furniture that we could not take.

The last engraving work for the company was my own selection. I withdrew a 338 Winchester barreled action out of the stockpile. Using the theme of Africa to draw inspiration from began engraving … I had decorated the floor plate with a Zulu shield pierced by a spear. Inlaid small mirror images of antelope and gazelle in gold on the receiver and had begun engraving the barrel when the Custom Shop supervisor Bruno Pardee stopped by. He looked at the job; suddenly there was interest in the rifle. A special stock blank was fitted, checkered, and finished for it. The company was to auction it off at the Safari Club International show in Las Vegas that January. I was quite pleased with myself, so pleased in fact that hidden on the underside of the barrel I engraved my name, which when discovered was promptly ground off.

Then it happened, Bruno came into the engraving room and told me what to do. He came into the work area and said

"We don't recognize the animals on the top of the receiver; put some detail in so that they look real."

I politely explained to Bruno that the figures were only elegant decorative shapes, artistic forms not animals. He told me that he wanted detail

I answered back "If I had wanted detail I would have put detail, and if he wasn't happy he could find another engraver to do it for him" It was to be the final engraved weapon done in the engraving room of the custom shop by me.

In those very first conversations with Mr. Hummel, I had asked him specifically,

"Was I was In charge of the engraving room?"

Carl's answer was, "That is the position I have hired you for Joseph."

From the first day, I started work at U.S. Repeating Arms Company I ran into trouble with the Union and its shop steward. It started when I wanted some chisel handles made, I was told to get a work order and wait in line like every one else. There were several engine lathes sitting idle, I found some brass bar stock, turned on the lathe and in thirty minutes, I had the handles, from that point forward things deteriorated

I still can recall my feelings of standing at the vise and imagining John and George Ulrich, Gough, Kusmet, Stokes, and other great engravers who stood as I did over the previous past 125 years. And seeing the treasures of other engravers lying in the cupboards and drawers, engraved bits and pieces of gun metal, sketches, engraving tools, partly finished print plates, wax impressions, all the collectable relics of the past engravers as I swept out the room, then closed the doors

U.S. Repeating Arms was failing as a company; after my departure, the engraving room shut its doors. The company also shut its doors not long after, filing for bankruptcy protection. I had achieved a small space in the history of firearms engraving. More importantly, I had finally managed to overcome my depression. .

The world of engraving is quite small.

There are perhaps 500 engravers that work in the United States, of which only a dozen or so are skilled enough to receive national recognition. It had taken me less than two years to achieve recognition in the engraving world.

Model 21 Grand American, bottom view

Chapter fourteen

"JOSEPH OF JOSEPH"

Thus, it was that Franca and I took off across country in the Ark, heading for Joseph, Oregon. Before leaving Connecticut, we reserved a post office box there.

I am sure the postmistress told everyone who walked in, that some fruitcake had rented a post office box insisting his name is Joseph, and only Joseph. Then I managed an interview with The New Haven newspaper, which included my post office box in Joseph, Oregon. We said our good byes to the few friends we had made.

Never having driven the Arc more than forty miles per hour, I had no way of knowing how it ran at higher speeds and loaded with cargo. We did not go but a few miles when it began to wallow and shimmy like a boat in a gale when its speed exceeded fifty miles per hour. I drove it that way until evening, when I stopped some where in Pennsylvania for the night; I found a mechanic, a motel, and a restaurant

The next morning with new shocks installed on the Ark, we were ready once again to sail forth across the greens, gold's, browns, and the grays of America. We were now united, Franca and I. Franca was my complete opposite; she found excitement in everything. With childlike enthusiasm, she watched out the windows as the miles carried us westward. That is until we entered the brown and flat part of the United States. Then she began worry.

"Where are the trees? I do not see any trees. Are there going to be trees in Oregon? I hope so. I wouldn't want to live somewhere where there are no trees."

"Don't worry. Babe, we'll have plenty of trees where we are going." I answered

The entire trip gave Franca a new impression of how expansive the land mass of the United States is. Finally interstate signs "Welcome to Oregon, Speed Limits Strictly Enforced, Buckle Up, Next Rest Area Nineteen Miles, Portland, 370 miles, drinking and Driving Will Cost Lives, Do Not Litter,

"Joseph I need to pee"

Our destination was La Grande, two hours down the interstate. Franca was oo-ing and ah-ing at the countryside passing by.

"Are there trees enough for you Babe" I smiled and took her hand in mine. We now had entered the russets, the gold's, the bright blue skies, mountains capped with snow and cascading rivers, all under one majestic sky.

"You know Franca; I can't help thinking that it's too bad Marcelle had not returned to France. That woman really scares me. Did I ever tell you about the time she tried to disembowel me with a big butcher knife?"

She tried to cut you, really.

I am serious, she attacked me in the kitchen of the home I built for my family, when we were once a family, and I was once a Dad …

"She hated you that badly?"

"I don't think she really hated me, she was sick, diagnosed as paranoid schizophrenic … I'm sure that she loved me in her own way. I told you that she came from a very mean family, that's the reason I fell in love with her, I felt sorry for her."

"You fell in love for one of the worst possible reasons there is," Amore.

"I under stand that now, but at eighteen I was so ignorant about life, when I saw how cruel her family was to one another. I felt that I had to save her, it's stupid I know."

"Its not stupid Joseph you did what you thought was right, that's all. I could not believe it when you told me the story of her brother skinning a mouse alive then letting it run across the kitchen floor."

"Its true, he had been in the French foreign legion, he stabbed her in her thigh with a fork one time. I saw him do it, they were the cruelest people I ever met, when I saw all that meanness I remembered my child hood and wanted to save her.

"That my dearest husband is another one of the worst reason to marry. You cannot change the way people are, if you love a person, you must love them as they are. How sad her life must have been, I feel sorry for her. Do you still love her?" She asked as she patted my hand."

"Franca, I will always love her, she bore my children, she kept us all clean and fed, she was strong and she loved her children as a lioness loves her cubs, Its all too sad. I don't wish to talk about it. It hurts too much.

You know I'm not looking forward to seeing her again, but as soon as we are settled in Joseph, I have to go and see my children"

"That's all right Amore, I do understand."

"I know babe, that's one of the one hundred reasons that I love you."

"You won't stop loving me? You do love me don't you Joseph, you wont drag me half way around the world then stop loving me. Promise me." I took her hand in mine.

"Franca how you could even consider such an idea, you know that no one in this world can separate me from you.

You know that I believe that destiny caused us to meet. I promise you babe. I can also promise you that if you or I ever are unhappy with each other our marriage will not endure." She said, "I understand that Joseph and I can accept that risk."

"Franca, I promise to you three things. I will never lie to you for any reason, that I will never hit you or yell at you, and I will always treat you with care and respect. But, there is one thing I can't promise."

"What is that Joseph?"

"I cannot promise you fidelity, I know myself too well to make you a promise that I could never keep under certain circumstances."

"I know that all ready Joseph, you were unfaithful to me when you were in Dallas and I still married you, did I not? There is a huge difference between sex and love, once the zipper is down. But I will remain faithful to you."

"That's another of the one hundred reasons that I adore you so babe ... Yes I was. It was just a circumstantial thing,this woman I met at the exhibition asked me out dinner after the show on Saturday and one thing led to another, that's all there was to it."

"You don't have to say you are sorry Amore, I have had more than my share of adventures, and so many I can't remember them all. In Casa Blanca, I was nearly arrested. Did I tell you that I had a man in my hotel and the management called the police? My lover left before they arrived, can you imagine what would have happened to me in a Moslem country?" I said, "That is one of the hundred reasons that I adore you babe, your sense of adventure."

"Joseph?" "What is it dear?" "Tell me about the others."

"What others are you talking about Franca?"

"The other hundred things you love about me, I need to know. We are a long way from my homeland and I miss my family." I kissed her.

"Well babe I love you for your kindness, your generosity, your common sense, your laughter, your smile, the passion you have when we make love, the color of your eyes, the feel of lips when we kiss, the smell of your hair, the touch of your skin,"

"Amore lets stop at the next motel we see and spend the night"

"It's still early Babe"

"I know that very well Joseph." She said with a gleam in her eye. "Then you can tell me the rest of the hundred reasons that you love me",

"Sounds like an excellent plan to me Babe"

"Look over there!"

I slowed the Ark then pulled over to the side of the road. There, in a green field of alfalfa were perhaps one hundred deer, browsing, heads down, white tail tips flicking back and forth. I was very tired and had driven most of the way. After Italy, I never had the greatest confidence in my wife's driving ability. We watched for a long while, I rested my arm and neck muscles, Franca curled up close to me, we kissed long and sweet..

"Let's find that motel Joseph I am getting very randy. I can also see that you are too"

She squeezed me hard and gave me a wicked grin.

We spent a wonderful night in La Grande. Late that morning, after egg Mac muffins and coffee we left the high plains of Oregon and began our assent into the Blue Mountains of Walalla County. The town of Joseph lay only eighty-seven twisting miles from the nearest MacDonald's. Populated with one hundred sixty two hardy souls, elevation 6000 feet give or take a foot or two.

Past the vast expanses of golden fall wheat fields littered with combines, horses, and Angus cattle. Then into the timber and sagebrush, scented canyon of the Grande Rounde River the Ark carried us on our way

"What do you think Joseph is going to be like?"

"I really don't know Babe; for sure there are enough trees. It is beautiful here, look at that river, bet there are fish in those waters",

"I have never caught a fish in my life time, you know how to fish Joseph, and will you teach me how to fish?" Surprised at her request, I asked my child bride.

"Do you think that you would enjoy that Babe? I love to fish, did it since I was a child, used to go fishing with my grand father. He was part Indian. He, I, and my uncle Waldo would catch fish for fertilizer; I recall he would put a fish under each corn seed"

"Joseph my lover, I want to enjoy doing things with you. You are the light of my life. Of course, I want to go fishing, but I do not want catch fish and put them in a garden. I want prepare them for our dinner, yes it is very beautiful here"

"So are you Babe" Franca rolled down her window and let the fresh clean mountain air flow over us.

She said, "Can you smell the forest? It reminds me of when I was a little girl living with my mom and dad in Gardone. I used to go on the back of my fathers motorcycle, he would take me into the mountains in the summer time. We would stay in a tiny little cabin over the weekend. He would take his birds in cages with us, hang them from the trees, and then he would shoot birds that came to the lures. I was his bird dog, I loved to be with my dad, but I hated killing those poor little birds. They terrify me; I can't touch even a feather."

I decided now was not the ideal moment to mention that bird hunting was some thing I enjoyed. No point anyway, didn't own a shotgun, or a dog.

"I'll be glad to stop, it has been a long trip, and you must be tired. Would you like me to drive for a while, so you can relax a bit, amore?"

"No babe I am fine, I'm not the least tired, besides this road is dangerous, we'll be their in half an hour"

"It's that you don't trust my driving, I know."

I often tell people that riding with Franca at the wheel is an exciting experience.

Once, after we settled in Oregon there was the triple spin down that same highway, caused by an unexpected sheet of ice. The occasion was our first wedding anniversary, which falls on Valentine's Day. We decided to go to La Grande, have a good meal in a nice restaurant, and stay at the best place in town, big night to celebrate.

I had been recently criticizing Franca's driving skills. So wanting to show her that I did indeed trust her driving, I asked her. "Would you like to drive dear?"

She answered in surprise, "Do you really want me to?"

"Of course I do, I think you are a fine driver my dear", I sighed.

La Grande was some miles away; the roads were clear and not a great deal of snow had fallen. I settled uncomfortably into the passenger's seat of our newly purchased Plymouth Horizon, buckled the safety belt, checked to make sure it was snug, and sat stiff as stone trying to maintain a calm demeanor as Franca drove.

"Slow down Franca. You're going too fast," I said, as we entered a shaded curve.

That's all I had time to say when the car lost traction on a patch of ice. Helpless, I saw her overcorrect. We were now making 50 mile an hour loop the loops down the highway. I looked out my side window at the oncoming pickup truck.

Somehow, it missed us by inches. Somehow, we missed all the signposts and with a crunch plowed into a large soft snow bank. We were unharmed and the car showed no sign of damages. The driver of the pickup and I worked the car out of the pile of snow. I took over the wheel and we continued on to La Grande to have our dinner.

Chapter fifteen

"A STRUGGLE IN JOSEPH"

The big two-story house we had rented in the bright warm sunshine of fall became as cold as the farthest distance from the sun. Gone were the blue skies, replaced by washes of black crystallized flakes of rain. The house had a huge living room with a stone fireplace, a large plate glass window allowing me to have the necessary north light I needed to engrave. Then there was the wonderful view of an apple tree whose wizened fruit attracted deer, chickadees, sparrows, and jays. Oh, how nice that studio looked in the false warmth of early fall with its massive stone fireplace.

The day we rented Mrs. Kaiser's old house was one of mixed feelings. I was glad to have safely made the trip. Franca was already planning her sister Juliana's visit to our new home in America … We had saved a few thousand dollars to tide us over until all those promises of work came true. I was a freelance artist able now to create the beautiful things I saw in my mind. Now I could really see how far I could go in life.

The town of Joseph itself was a sad place, It was not important. Franca was with me, I would work, we could hike the moraine over looking the glacial Walalla Lake, fish the rivers together, picnics and horse back rides. I would live my life out there, fame and fortune would assuredly come. We would have guests/clients over for pizza, living in the land of milk and honey … The natural beauty was indescribable. The land there still shows nature's turmoil when the crystal waters of the lake were formed millions of years ago.

I met a man as I was moving in; he was moving out of a small house across the street. He was loading furniture as I was unloading mine.

I introduced myself.

"Are you moving out?" I asked curiously.

"Damn right," he replied.

"But how can you leave all this beauty? Look at those mountains, look at the clear skies. How can you leave?"

"You can't eat those friggin mountains boy, them there clear blue lakes, and skies makes damn thin soup." He turned his back and walked to his house for more things, muttering "goddamn idjit,"

Me returning to the toil of unloading the Ark, wondering, "What's bugging him?"

"Let no white man live on this land in peace. Whatever white man comes here to live, he shall die from the cold and hunger," said Joseph, Chief of the Nez Pierce.

Fall vanished, blown away by the north wind. The cold -10, -15, -20, -30 degrees, came in freezing waves, driving us out of the wonderful living room and my studio. At first, we fought it, building huge fires in the stone fireplace. Soon, the pitiful pile of wood reached bottom.

It was not long before I was spending all of my time salvaging firewood from the mountainous piles of scrap belonging to the local logging company. I would load the back of the Ark with all the wood that it could haul, return to our big house, unload, split it, stack it, and return for more. Franca meanwhile, was feeding it into the fireplace almost as fast as I could split it.

I could not keep up. Needed a chainsaw, went to a local dealer asked if he would like to make a trade—some engraving on his rifle for a chainsaw. He opted for an elk in profile on one side of his Browning automatic rifle. I chose a Home Light with a twenty-four inch cutting bar. I was now risking life and limb to keep us from freezing.

Winter deepened, we retreated, and the studio became so cold that I could not touch my vise. It was now a block of frozen steel. I relocated into the laundry room, where there was no view and poor light, but at least there was a semi-efficient baseboard heater. We hung blankets over the doors, bought an electric blanket for our upstairs love nest. I stopped sleeping nude, bought thermal underwear. I was so tired at the end of the day, that the love nest had become simply "the nest." The cold had become so intense that we would wear coats, hats, and gloves in the house. Franca's glass of milk froze on her nightstand.

One-day, years later, we were having our usual dinner conversation when I brought up the subject of the cold of Joseph, Oregon.

"I never told you," she said. "But when we were in Joseph, Oregon, and you were working at gun shows every weekend. I sort of hoped that you would die and maybe I could return to Italy as a widow"

I rather felt likewise about the situation. To say that Joseph was a terrible town would be unfair, but I do believe it would make a wonderful witness protection community.

Joseph and Franca, Joseph—Oregon

It was late January when the Ark finally collapsed into a pile of worn-out junk, money was starting to run low. The abandonment of the Ark meant that we needed new wheels. I went to the used car dealer in the town of Enterprise, found a small front wheel drive with a standard transmission. Franca hates automatic transmissions, claims she has "no control of the car." Its purchase price wiped out our cash reserve. We were down to what my engraving skills would earn. The promises that were in the post office box turned out to be just that. The first time I went to the newly rented and advertised box it was stuffed with letters, which Franca answered, sending out price lists and photos to the return addresses.

"What the hell did he do? Change his name when he got to the town limits?" The locals would say behind our backs.

"What about that foreign wife of his? They say she speaks 'Aitalian.'"

Joseph was not a kind town but we did not mind. We had each other.

Franca took over the responsibilities of answering the enquiries that came. UPS rarely stopped at the door. At some point, I had to ask the local grocer to credit me a box of pasta and a tin of tomatoes. It was $1.85, if I recall correctly.

There is a saying in the town of Joseph "Once you enter Walalla County, you never leave, for you can never earn enough money to get back out again."

I had finished the proto type Whitney rifle sending it back to Mister Lindsey. In due, time his check came, along with a letter from his widow. He had died never seeing the work, circumstances dictating the canceling of the project. This was a huge disappointment, but I never let setbacks keep me from loosing faith in my journey through life. I knew that I was to master my destiny, even though I was not sure what that destiny was to be.

Engraving commissions were non-existent. In order to maintain and improve my skills, I began engraving intaglio plates. The prints themselves I found saleable. These plates brought me a small but regular income over the next twenty years.

I started going to local gun shows and would set up vise, tools and examples of my work, engrave on the spot. Initials: $2 a letter, kids pocket knives free. I had to stop doing that when one time in Montana I looked up from the work to see a line of waiting kids twenty feet long I have no idea how many pocket knives I have put initials in, several hundred at least. I also engraved pistols on the spot; I would walk up and down the aisles of the gun show looking for stainless steel Smith and Wesson, or Ruger handguns.

Then ask the owners "would you like that engraved"?

They would generally say no. Then ask out of curiosity, how much? Depending on my desperation, I would quote a price of thirty to a hundred fifty dollars

If I had made a sale, I would secure the gun in my vise, work rapidly cutting with out drawing a design first, reducing my work time by almost half. By my third year as engraver I could cut simple designs almost as fast with a chisel as I could draw them with a pencil, thanks to Senor Roberto Aquilari's advise.

Model 94/22, top view of frame.

I would finish the job in thirty or forty minutes, put it away, find another pistol, and do the same thing again. Then after two or three hours, return the first gun to its owner. He would happily pay me, believing that I had worked that amount of time on his weapon. Meanwhile, the tapping of the hammer would draw a crowd of onlookers and perhaps I would pick up a decent commission that would allow me to show off all my skills. At one of these shows, I sold the beautiful 22 rifle Franca had designed.

I was desperate for cash, very happy for the sale. My commissions started to increase and we were out of danger.

One of my clients asked me to engrave a Colt pistol for him. He wanted a modest amount of my finest work. Not only was it a good commission, it was also informative.

"Did I know about the Buffalo Bill Museum in Cody Wyoming?" He asked

"No, I had never heard of it," I replied.

"I was recently there, in the engraved gun section, I saw a rifle that you had engraved at the factory. It is on display and gives you credit for the engraving."

I absorbed this for a moment and then almost breathlessly said, "Wow."

Soon afterward, I contacted the museum and talked with the curator, a Mr. Herbert Houze. I asked what rifle was on display. He told me it was a Model 94 Carbine purchased for the museum while he was in Dallas. I knew exactly what gun he was talking about. It was the second rifle of my career. I had developed skills way past that level at this point and I asked if he would be interested in purchasing another rifle I had just finished.

The conversation ended on a positive note. Mr. Houze asked me to ship him the rifle. [You could do that once in America.] Franca packaged the gun up with her usual care and shipped the gun off.

Model 94 Big Bore Winchester, work in progress

I waited two weeks and not being able to stand the suspense any longer, I called Mr. Houze again.

"Yes," he had the rifle and "did I have any other works?" I said I had a rifle floor plate and trigger guard, inlaid with a gold ibex's head.

He then told me that Christy's were holding an auction that July and he would personally see that the auction catalogue included the rifle and the other pieces.

That summer, Franca and I received a formal invitation to the Buffalo Bill Historical Center.

It was a long three months before the auction. We were out of Mrs. Kaiser's big house with the great studio, into a much smaller and warmer cottage.

The studio was a heated extra bedroom, with the closet serving as engraving space. I was doing a lot of soul-searching while living in Joseph. I had gone to visit my children soon after I had dependable transportation again. I found everything completely out of control. None of them attended school any longer. My daughter Lisa had a child out of wedlock. Mark the oldest son was living in a room with squalor. Allan was living with a girlfriend and having emotional problems. Joss the second daughter had recently married. Diana the youngest daughter was afflicted with anorexia. Only Joe the youngest son seemed to have escaped the judge's decision. Marcelle had gotten worse in the passing years.

First, I talked to Mark, the oldest. "Come live with me. I am your father. I can teach you, you can walk over all of the obstacles I went through to learn the trade."

"I'm not interested," he replied. "I want to be an auto mechanic. Besides where were you when I needed you?"

Lisa, the eldest daughter, had bonded to her mother's side. She and my granddaughter were totally under Marcelle's control.

Next, I talked to my son Allen. "Come live with me," I begged. "I want to help you. I can teach you this trade. You can make a good living, be respected."

"That sounds cool. Why not? Can Linda also go?" Linda was Allen's first love. He called her 'Pumpkin.'

Son, "If you come with me, you come alone. I cannot teach you and have you distracted by 'Pumpkin."

"Well, can I take my car?"

He had recently bought a Ford Torino. It was a powerful, good-looking auto, painted yellow and black. I could not handle "Pumpkin's" presence, but I could tolerate the car.

Next, I tried to convince Diana, to come away with me, but she did not wish to leave her mother or sister. Joe, my youngest son was still in school and in the custody of his mother. Therefore, I took what I could salvage and headed back East to Joseph, with Allen's Torino headlights in my rear view mirror.

The ever-gracious Franca greeted Allen with warmth and love. Happily, I started my son on drawing lessons and was pleased to note he had a natural instinct for design and form. He always had a good sense of humor as a child but after a few days with Franca and me, we began to notice that he had many peculiar traits. He would disappear after his supper and return late. If I did not insist that he get out of bed, he would stay there until hunger got him up.

He had available to him quite a bit of cash. Franca and I discussed this issue and decided to ask Allen about his life. He told us that he had quit school at 16 and said for the last couple of years he had been living with an old widow who had a house near the Willamette River. He took care of the chores and she gave him money, enough he said, to buy the Torino with cash.

Had he ever been in trouble with the law? I wanted to know.

"Yes," he replied. "I was picked up by the police in Oregon City."

"What in the world for?" I asked.

He said, "They said that I killed an old woman, but there was no body so eventually they let me go."

I did not know what to say so I continued as if nothing of importance had occurred.

"What did you do with it?" I asked calmly as I could.

"I think I cut it up and I threw it in the Willamette River. I really don't remember."

"Oh," was all I could say.

Allen looked at me, gave me a flashing smile, then said, "Just kidding, Dad."

"Well son I think I'm ready for bed. Goodnight, I'll see you in the morning."

"Goodnight, Dad. I love you."

Good night son, I love you also."

"Are you also ready for bed?" I asked Franca.

"I was just going," she quickly replied.

Later in bed, Franca and I discussed this remarkable conversation late into the night. We decided that we could say no more about it. It was not but a few days later, Pumpkin showed up, driven there by her parents. I could sense Franca's unhappiness with the whole situation.

The training of Allen had come to a standstill. It was not long before I watched the taillights of the Torino turn onto the main street of Joseph and disappear, headed back to Portland.

That left Joe, the youngest son. I decided to kidnap him. I went to Portland leaving Franca alone to brave the loneliness and cold.

I went to Joe's school and talked with the principal and his teachers. They implored me to get him out of there, away from his environment.

I then conspired with a couple of old friends to have Joe visit them with their children after school. I went to the police and told them what I planned to do, just to see how much trouble I could get into. It seemed like it was going to be a lot.

I picked up Joe's school records and then went to get Joe. He was afraid, and close to tears when I explained what I was about to do. However, after a long and patient talk I finally convinced him to come with me. Once settled and on our way across the state, Joe took notice of the countryside while I drove in silence, my mind racing with thoughts.

"My son, I've got you now. I loved you and I missed you. You were never out of my mind all these years." All the while I am thinking, I was checking my rear view mirror, expecting the Oregon highway patrol to stop me.

Our trip home was uneventful and we arrived to find Franca waiting with open arms and a beautiful smile. I had called ahead and she had prepared a pizza for Joe's arrival. For the days of Joe's stay, my heart would jump every time a car drove by the yard. Then we went hiking alone on the moraine overlooking the town of Joseph and the lake. I can still remember him sliding down the snowy slopes, cheeks pink, blue eyes flashing in happiness. I began to relax. I recall also us skating together and fishing through the ice. I began to believe I could be a father again. It was at the end of his first week with us that there was a knock on the door. I opened it and came face to face with Marcelle and Lisa. Poor Marcelle, age had taken its toll. She looked shrunken, lost. I looked at her realizing that my dreads had arrived.

"How did you find me? How did you get here without killing yourselves in a wreck?" I could not keep the disappointment from showing.

Marcelle had gotten her driver's license on her third attempt.

"How did you get here?" I finally managed to say again.

"Lisa drove," she replied.

"Oh," I did not argue. I knew why she had come, knew I could not win, had tried but I was beaten.

"Joe, your mother's here to take you home."

Goodbye, my ten-year-old son with a flashing smile and a sly look of curiosity, I did not see him again until eight years later. From my diary:

March 9, 1984

My youngest son has come and gone. I had him with me but for four days. I am so sad to see him go. For I know he is lost to me forever. Never will I have the inner glow of pride, that a father must feel when he sees his own flesh and blood accomplish a difficult task, learn something new, take pride in himself.

Chapter sixteen

"RECOGNITION"

It was at this distressing time that I received my first important commission. Olin Corporation contacted me to engrave for them a Model 101 shotgun with a theme of the Statue of Liberty being central to the project that they intended to present to Lee Iacocca and use as a fundraiser for the Statue of Liberty's renovation going on at that time. I began working on the preliminary drawings of the vignette. After considerable research at the public library, finally found the scene I wanted. It was the railing of a ship lined with immigrants looking at the distant outline of the statue of liberty.

The space I had for such a scene was about two square inches. For clarity, I did the drawings four times actual size. The drawings took ten days to complete. I included Franca as one of the passengers leaning over the railing. I sent the drawing by mail, giving the postmistress a smug smile as I did so. The phone rang five days later. It was Olin Corporation. Yes, they had the drawings and they were more than satisfied with them. The secretary would mail a check out right away to pay for the artwork, and the gun would follow.

"Oh, Hallelujah and Amen" I thought.

The project never went any further than the drawings; nevertheless, it would have been a magnificent gun. I have engraved many magnificent guns during my career, but very few were commissions. I had problems with commission work as most of the clients wanted relatively simple engraving and I wanted to make masterpieces. One exception being Mr. Leon Wandler of Gillette Wyoming who gave me several fine Winchester 1873 and 1876 rifles to engrave in the following years

The time finally arrived for Franca and I to make our drive out to Cody, Wyoming. As we drove, we speculated on what would happen at the Buffalo Bill Historical (B.B.H.C.) and the Christy's auction.

We arrived late next evening, found a motel, got something to eat and fell asleep exhausted. Cody City was not the same Cody I had driven through thirty years earlier with Marcelle and my first two children. Where there had been dirt streets and narrow roads, there were now highways and neat avenues with the Buffalo Bill Historical Center standing impressively on the curve of the highway leading to Yellowstone Park. In the morning I walked from the motel to the B.B.H.C. went to the security desk, signed in the registry and waited for Mr. Houze.

After handshakes and hellos, he invited me to take the tour of the Winchester arms collection. There were many hundreds of different types of weapons, but on that particular day, my interest focused on the one that said, "Engraved by Joseph."

When Mr. Houze stopped in front of the glass display case containing the rifle, my heart swelled with pride. I knew that I would make it. That I would leave a small but tangible mark on this world and perhaps one of my children or great grandchildren would take pride in the art I had created. After the tour, Mr. Houze took me up the stairs to where the review for the auction was going on. Again, there were many beautiful and interesting weapons, but my eyes searched the gun racks, looking for the model Winchester 94.

I had spent many hours working on it, taken it apart, and put it back together so many times; I could recognize that gun from fifteen feet away. I asked the man who was handling the preview if I could handle that rifle.

"Would you mind putting these on, sir?" he said handing me a pair of spotless white gloves.

I thought, "How strange that these hands with the calluses and stained fingernails need to be gloved to handle the finished work." I smiled and put on the gloves and enjoyed looking at the rifle.

"What do you think this rifle will bring?" I asked, I was so curious and excited I could hardly stand it.

"I can't really say sir. It's a beautiful piece of work and it should do well." Satisfied with the answer I left the preview and returned to give Franca the good news. That night and the following Sunday morning we speculated on what the rifle might bring. I was hoping for around $3000. We were again short of money and needed the auction to go well.

The auction room was empty when we arrived; we were almost an hour early. Soon all the seats were full. We sat in the very back of the room holding hands, waiting for my work to come on the block. The first piece up was the gold inlaid floor plate and trigger guard. The price quickly rose as several bidders vied for the work. The bidding ended at $1500. Now we were excited. Next the rifle, came up to the auctioneers block To our surprise the opening bid was $2500, escalating quickly to $3500, then $4500, then $6500, then $7500, then $8000, where the bidding ended. We were deliriously happy. We went out to celebrate that evening. Franca liked Cody, as did I.

On the return trip to Joseph, we discussed moving to Wyoming. I felt that the B.B.H.C. would be a good springboard to launch my career. What better references could I ask for? Graduate of one of the finest schools of engraving in the world, Master Engraver at the Winchester custom shop. Work in the firearms collection of the Buffalo Bill Historical Center. All that accomplished in less than three years. We arrived home, tired and happy, were greeted by our tomcat named Tiger. Tiger was the first pet to enter our lives and we became strongly attached to him.

Time went by slowly as we waited for the check to arrive. It was at that time that we were at our lowest on cash. Finally a letter with the check for the floor plate and trigger guard arrived but not the one for the rifle. I waited another week, but no check. In desperation, I called Mr. Houze. There was a glitch in the sale he explained, the last bidder having reneged on the bid. The rifle remained unsold. I was disappointed, but at least I had gotten some good exposure and still had the rifle to sell. I also had a much clearer idea of what my work was worth. The disappointments for my children were very bitter pills to swallow. For the previous five years, my only goal had been to become famous as an engraver and to open a school. I felt that my life's experiences held some value and I would make a good teacher. I really wanted to help my children.

I was completely wrong about myself and wrote in my journal, "As for teaching I will share and have shared all my life up to this point, but from now on forget about it. I'm going to dedicate my life to making beautiful works, and if the rest of the world wants to go its way that's ok."

Memorial Afternoon (From my journal)

Well folks, here is the rest of the story as Paul Harvey says. Lunch was wonderful, bean soup and half a sandwich. Bought a new fly rod, the first good one I had since I closed the door on the place I was living in Virginia, leaving everything behind, clothes, car, furniture, stereo, last name, runaway life and a second wife. Franca and I spent the afternoon fishing. I have sunburns. More news, yesterday I received a verbal commitment from the B.B.H.C. for a commission, from Olin Corporation. I also finished a piece of work for the Kimber's Arm Company that they will display at the NRA show. Not long ago, I finished one for the Eli Whitney museum, so things are going well and I am two years ahead of my schedule.

As I said, I do not see life through the eyes of others.

[I think that when someone truly intends to take their own life and only by a miracle fails, that person views of what is important in life, change dramatically, forever.]

What I cherished most while living with Franca in Joseph, Oregon were the memories of us on the rivers fishing. I had a person to share life with I could trust. I could open that sack of secrets, fears, and sadness to her and know I was safe from pain.

When I met Franca, I was like a wild wolf. I was distrustful, had horrible and bloody nightmares, was prone to long bouts of depression, and had just about rejected people from my life. With her love and honesty, I became well. I could laugh again. I slept soundly at her side. I no longer would wake with a pounding heart, or start screaming or crying. I had conquered my life.

Although Joseph was not good to us financially, the natural beauty was abundant. Franca had never been fishing before in her entire life. Her childhood had been spent hiking in the mountains with her dad and vacationing on the seaside with her aunts. Then skiing and tennis became her favorite sports when she grew older. She had schooled in Cambridge, England, then as an adult, traveled the world selling cargo containers of plumbing fittings in Africa, United Arab Emirates, Europe, Hong Kong, Singapore and other places. She traveled first class always, a man in every port my travels, although extensive, were completely different. Her sister Giuliana refers to me as Joseph, the barbarian.

After the purchase of the fly rod came a spinning rod for Franca. Equipped with our new gear, we set off to go fishing. Franca was dressed in a spotless white jumpsuit, new white tennis shoes. I was in my usual jeans and shirt.

I shall always retain the image of my child bride dressed in white. She had a little red make-up bag that she had converted into a worm container by tying a piece of red ribbon to it around her neck. Not wanting her to get dirty or scratched, I decided to fish next to a busy bridge where the footpath to the water would be well worn and safe.

We parked our newly purchased Horizon, and then went on our expedition. The path was safe enough all right, but the heavily fished spot did not offer any luck. I was sure that if we walked upstream a ways we would find better.

"Come on dear," I said. "Let's go somewhere else. I'll lead and you follow." Taking her hand, I began to break away the brush and brambles to clear a passage for her. I found a less-fished spot up stream. I instructed her how to bait the hook, and how to cast, showed her where to throw the bait and in a few seconds she was hooked to a small rainbow trout. In quick succession, she caught three or four more. The fish stopped biting after a while.

Then, she said, "Let's go upstream a little further. I'm having so much fun. I love you" She smiled.

"This is another one of the hundred reasons I adore you too, babe," I said with a joyous grin.

Soon we were in a lovely meadow with silver cottonwoods growing along the rivers banks, their shadows making inviting places to sit while I watched her fish, and living was easy.

I stopped paying attention to Franca and continued upstream looking for another spot that would hold more fish, leaving her some twenty yards behind me, proudly carrying four little fishes on a forked stick … I came to a small stream about two feet wide and three inches deep with crystal water running through it. Normally I would have stepped into it without thinking a thing about it. So happened that lying across the stream was a tree limb as big around as my wrist. For fun, I decided to see if I could walk the branch. Tripping the light fantastic across the branch without ever getting my feet wet, I looked back and saw Franca was close by and approaching the small stream. I turned and started scouting the river again.

Suddenly she was screaming, "Aiuto, aiuto, aiuto! Help me! Help me!" I dropped my new fly rod, and then went racing toward the sound of her screams. Then I saw her in the center of that innocent looking stream, covered above those beautiful breasts in black, stinking muck. She was standing there holding the stick with the little fishes above her dark brown hair. My heart sank. I started to reach for her to help her out.

"No," she insisted. "I'm all right. Take my fish." I took the fish, dragging her out of the mud as gently as I could I helped her to the river where she stripped off her cloths and washed the mud away from her lithe body.

"Franca, you look like a wood nymph, let's go home, and make love," I teased while helping her into my shirt.

She was shivering; her lips were blue, goose bumps over body. She kissed me and said, "That's a wonderful idea Joseph, but first I think we should do it here."

To say that I love her is an understatement. Later when she had more experience, she was willing to fish more dangerous waters. She never failed to listen to my instructions and to trust me completely. Soon, she was leading the way over branches and boulders, searching the icy currents of cascading liquid for a spot that might contain her next fish.

Franca makes a baked wild trout stuffed with herbs, peas, and ham that is to die for. It was in Joseph that my wife discovered the pleasures of cooking. She started baking pastries, breads, and selling them to the bookstore in Enterprise. I made a sign for the kitchen with some rag paper and watercolors, "Franca's Pastries and Breads" surrounded by bouquets of roses.

It was 1985. There was a warming sun and the air was cobalt blue. The ice had begun to shrink away from Walalla lake's edges. We decided to go up to the lake and fish for a bit, but mostly just to enjoy the sun and the day together.

Easter Sunday (from my journal)
Many vows I have made to you and many vows I will break. You made me, Lord. I am your greatest mistake. Many offers I have made to you with deep sincerity of heart and many times I have gone back on my word yet you trust me Lord and for that, I make you this sword. You sent your son to watch us grow. We destroyed him with one mighty blow. With regret, I engrave this plate. For you love him as you love me. I am so sorry. But this I know you know. Please help me and forgive us all, for you made us. No doubt your greatest mistake.

With leaves of rust,
The green plants droop,
Standing guard by the decaying stoop,
With branches growing in deformity,
On the perimeter of my home,
A lonely elm stands guard,
There so lost and alone
They are the protectors,
The keepers of my house,
But I man have failed them
And given them a curse of blight,
I'm sorry please forgive me,
For I didn't have that right,
Slowly I watched them shriveling, curling up and dying,
Disappearing in smoke before my eyes.

The town of Joseph was and, I am sure, still is, a mystical spot. It was during our stay in Joseph that I started writing more often in my journal. I really do not know why. I suppose it had to do with the area's Indian history.

Joseph was a place where I had my first encounter with a full-blooded Indian. It was also, where a very unusual thing happened.

I had taken a sketchpad and a few colored pencils with me, then went hiking by myself around the terrain surrounding Walalla Lake, now called Chief Joseph Lake. I was sitting on a knoll overlooking a small dam, doing nothing in particular, just watching a red-tailed hawk soaring in the rising air currents.

After the hawk had drifted away, my gaze settled back down on the small valley below. I started looking at the patterns of the boulders laid out on the lovely valley floor. Studying them carefully, something artistic people do, I began to see there was logic in their placement.

"It looks like teepee rings," I thought.

The more I studied the stones, the surer I was that someone had put them there. I got up and made my way down the hill to those circles of rocks.

Once there, I started studying them close up. Three of the stone rings were round. One was elliptical; it was the largest, at least twenty feet long and ten feet wide. The boulders around the outside were pumpkin-size. With the exception of two very large stones set about three feet apart. "Looks like an entrance to me," I decided.

I started to enter the stone circle. As clear as the cry of the red tail hawk I had been watching, a voice said,

"Take off your boots."

Without hesitation, I removed the boots and stepped inside the grassy ring.

First, I saw a large fire-blackened stone abutted to the entrance stone on the left. Arranged around the blackened stone were several smaller flat ones. I stood there, not moving, just taking everything in. Then noticed a dozen seat-sized stones arranged in a semi-circle. I sat down on one to see if it was comfortable. It was comfortable, as comfortable as a rock can possibly be. I sat taking in the feeling of the place, as I did; I happened to notice that the rock near by the entrance was very sharp and looked to be the most uncomfortable rock anyone could have sat on. Just to make sure, I changed seats. About two minutes, was all the pain I could stand. I walked out of the ring of stones, put on my boots thinking, "This can't be a teepee ring. No one would sit on a stone that painful."

Once again, I heard the voice. It said, "That stone was placed for the white man when he came to my lodge."

When I returned home from my hike, I told Franca the whole story. She listened enthusiastically but I could tell she had her doubts.

"Have you been smoking that stuff **again**?"

I admitted that yes, I had smoked a **bit** while enjoying my walk.

"I think perhaps you were a bit **intoxicated** and if you go there again you won't hear voices."

The matter of spirits settled, she kissed me and we had lunch. Later that same month our cat Tiger disappeared. He was a tom and often disappeared for a day or so but a week had passed. Franca was very concerned; we would walk the town streets and alleys calling his name. By the end of the week, I was so sure that someone had killed him, I wrote in my journal:

"Daylight plays across the mantle,
In reds, greens, and gold,
The flowers that are growing there look beautiful,
Surely, I am growing old.
My cat, he used to warm himself
In that little spot of sun.
But now he's gone forever more
The victim of my neighbor's gun.
And deep inside I feel the pain
Of another empty space,
Mankind has struck again,
Leaving loneliness in its place.
Surely I am growing old."

Perhaps it was the disappearance of Tiger that brought back sad, long buried remembrances of my youth, my stepfather Ernest, and a dog I once loved named Frenchy. I was thirteen. One day as I got off the school bus, Ernest was waiting for me holding his twenty two-caliber rifle in one hand,

"Here" he said. "Take this, your dog, your damn dog went up to the neighbor's farm and killed two of his chicken. Had to pay him 25 cents apiece, damn dog cost me fifty cents.
Do you know how hard I work for fifty cents?" he yelled.
"No sir," I replied, my heart pounding in trepidation, as I had felt the sting of his wrath many times before.
"Now you take that damn dog down to the woods and shoot it and bury it." He cuffed me upside of the head, shoved the rifle in my hand saying "now get to it boy."
What could I do? He was adamant, and I was just a boy.
"Yes sir," I said and went to where he had tied up my dog to a tree, took the rope off his neck, "Come Frenchy, let's go."

Over half a century has passed and I can still see Frenchy running along the path, left by the ditch that I had dug, that led to the well and onto the logging road.

A giant oak marked one of the boundaries of Ernest LaVarnois's 35 acres of hardwood and pine. It was the largest oak tree on the property. It had been on this earth before the stonewalls marking the boundaries were built. It was so large that its girth extended out beyond the width of the stone- wall by several feet.

It was my favorite place to play. I had nailed pieces of woods to its trunk so that I could climb up into the huge comforting branches. Frenchy was busily searching for the scent of a squirrel in front of me, his white feet running through the fallen oak leaves. The tip of his tail waving back and forth about twenty feet in front of me. When we reached the oak, I called "Frenchy." He stopped and turned to look at me.

I put the cross hairs of the rifle on a spot centered between his trusting eyes and pulled the trigger. He fell to the ground, his legs kicking, his body jerking. I ran to him, tears bursting forth, and ever-mounting misery consuming me.

Through blurry eyes I could see my dog laying on the ground, blood coming from his mouth and ears, urine on his legs, mouth curled in pain. "He is not dead," I thought, for I had not seen death before. I thought the final convulsions indicated life. I had no strength left to shoot him again. I placed my foot upon his throat and pressed with all my might, eventually his quivering subsided and his eyes glazed over. He had trusted me, loved me, I had murdered him. I sat with him a long time, hating myself and the world I knew. When my well of tears had emptied and my limbs had regained their strength, I lifted his body, carried him to my favorite place in the woods.

There, under that ancient oak whose bent and twisted limbs I had climbed many times spying for Indians and hunting for squirrels, I buried him. Frenchy was only three years old when I murdered him.

He was my friend. We ran together in the woods. We wrestled under the pines where the silver brown needles made a fragrant mat for us to roll on. He was my dog; I loved him, I shot him.

I sat there at the base of that gnarled oak for a long time, a confused, sad, hurt, lonely boy. Finally, I got to my feet, finished snuffling and crying, and slowly walked home.

That experience instantly aged me; I remember that incident at other times in life, for it has softened me as the years have gone by. The anger has disappeared and in its place is a strange sort of love, for now I can better appreciate how gentle animals are to each other. How plants survive so harmoniously. How innocent small children are. I have the deepest love for a flower, yet I have a great disdain for the adult human race as a majority.

These were the thoughts on my mind when we started preparing for our departure from the town of Joseph, Oregon. Needing money, I took the unsold rifle to the bank, along with the Christie's catalogue listing it, explained about the glitch in the sale, and asked to use it for loan collateral. The president of the bank looked the rifle over and approved a loan of $2,000, payable in full six months hence. With that, we paid off the car and started our moving sale. This is when our brush with the Walalla County law began. Actually, it began on our arrival.

Big people in small towns do not care for small people with ideas in their towns. In the short time that we had lived there, I had managed to get involved with a fundraising project. A rifle with Chief Joseph's portrait was going to be raffled off. The Chamber of Commerce commissioned the engraving. Then I got involved with selling of raffle tickets at the gun show circuits I was traveling in, those days I traveled a lot.

The agreement with the Chamber of Commerce was, I would sell tickets and display the rifle. They, in return, would give me forty percent of the sales. I would attend a show in Boise, Idaho, the following Friday, Saturday, and Sunday. We agreed to try out the raffle at that show. There I sold fifty tickets at ten dollars a piece. When I returned home, I contacted Bub, the cheese chief of the Chamber of Commerce and gave him his portion of the receipts. Suddenly he started complaining about the percentages.

I held up my hand; he shut up. I handed him the rifle, the tickets, the stubs and $300 in cash, then showed him the door saying.

"Get out of this house. I have better things to do with my time than screw around with you."

A short while later came the local art show. I had finished an ink rendering of the old boots I had worn to Italy, the ones that had killed my feet; along with a cowboy hat. The drawing took a bit of time and as I sketched the boots, I recalled that trip to Italy. When the drawing was finished, I took the worn out boots and dropped them in the dumpster in the alley.

I reserved the space at the local art show in the town of Enterprise, hoping to run into a potential engraving client. I decided to frame the boots drawing and hang it at the show. It needed a title. I could see no sense in a title such as "Old Friends" or "The Last Mile." "The Boots that I Suffered With" didn't seem quite right either. Therefore, I entitled it "Shitkickers and a Fly Swatter," signed it, framed it, and left it with the Walalla county art league secretary. I found it the afternoon of the first showing, hanging at the back of the show near the men's urinal. It is now in the permanent collection of the B.B.H.C ...

Franca and I were taking our usual evening walk after dinner. Up the cold, dismal, lonely, empty streets of Joseph. She noticed a small restaurant for sale called The Blue Moon Café.

"Oh, amore," she asked as we walked by. "Do you think I could ever have a little restaurant?"

Her question interrupted my thoughts of how poorly I was doing. I had my arm around her shoulder and stopped to give her a tight hug and a light kiss.

"I don't think so; I don't think we will ever have the money, dear." We resumed our walk.

I knew that the town of Joseph had a local poker game every Friday night at the Frontier Bar. A retired Merchant Marine named Ed run it in a back corner. The players were all local businessmen and the occasional fish that flopped in the door; I decided to see if I could win some extra cash. The first time I played, I lost some $25 getting to know the game. The night ended and everyone asked me back to play again.

"See you next Friday!" Ed said as I walked out the door.

"You come back now!" The rest of the players all chimed in.

The following Friday, again I lost a small amount.

"We'll send a taxi for you next time," Ed, joked as I got up from the table to leave.

Franca, who had accepted the idea of my gambling with our meager resources, started voicing her concerns. "Amore, Are you sure?"

"Next time, I will win," I reassured her.

The following Friday I was ready to play poker. By the time the bar closed, I had several hundred dollars of Ed's money and several hundred more of the other players. Usually the game ended at closing time, but that night it went on until daybreak.

I returned home to find Franca sleeping. I took the stack of bills from my pocket and laid them out on the living room floor, spelling out the words 'I love you' in fives, tens, twenties, fifties and hundred dollar bills, got into bed, kissed her neck and started to go to sleep.

"Did we win?" she asked sleepily.

"Si, Stella," I whispered to her. "Go back to sleep." I never received another invitation to the game.

I decided it was time to say good-by to Joseph, Oregon and move to Cody, Wyoming. Franca cheerfully agreed.

We were about finished with our moving sale when the local real estate agent showed up

"I think you owe me a month's rent," he said after stepping out of his car. No 'hello,' no pleasant inquiries, just a demand for money. Franca joined my side.

"We do not owe you money," she said with finality. "The house has been sold as of a month ago and if money is owed, it is to the new owner, not to you."

My wife has a way of seeing through frauds and she was sure that the realtor intended to pocket the money for himself.

"Yes, you do," the realtor insisted. "And (sound familiar?) I'm going to call the sheriff." He turned back to his car, and then drove away.

Thunderheads had been darkening all afternoon, lightning split them open, heavy snow laden rain began to fall. I had almost finished packing the car; the house was now clean and empty. Raindrops pelting on the top of my naked head, I went dashing back into the house to gather up the remains of our personal things, back out through the storm again yelling to Franca, "Find the cat!" She found Tiger and came to the door.

"I've got him. What do you want me to do?"

"Put the cat in the car and let's get the hell out of here!" I yelled as I opened the passenger side door for her and the cat, shut it firmly, ran around to the driver's side, soaking wet and shivering, started the fully loaded car, put it in gear and headed down toward the Snake River Canyon and back roads that would take us into Idaho, Montana and Wyoming.

From my journal, May 31st

Down the road we go. We adventurous three,
Franca, Tiger and me,
With $600 in cash, bills paid,
The Idaho sun shining down on us adventurous three,
We escaped from the sheriff of Wallala County. Went out the back way, we're on our way to Wyoming. To have our day with destiny,
Franca Tiger and me.

June 2, 1985
On the road, Wyoming is beautiful. I hope it's better to us than Joseph was.
I fell in love with the beauty of Joseph, but that is like marrying (as Franca says) beauty with a cold heart and a mean tongue.

Chapter seventeen

"HAVE HAMMER WILL TRAVEL"

We arrived in Cody on June 3, 1985. Found a small upstairs, over the garage, in the back, next to the alley, furnished apartment. Cody has many alley apartments, all with a fraction attached to the principle dwellings number. Most of all the "halfs" in Cody are recognized by their address; life is tough on the *one-halfs,* Franca and I were "halfs" our first time in Cody.

Once our housing needs were secure, we had the time to check out the town, buy food for us, and Tiger the cat, and then unwind.

Dressed in my rarely worn charcoal grey wedding suit, strolling next morning through the town that Buffalo Bill Cody founded. Gave me the time to think about that museum and its vast treasures of handcrafts, sculptures, paintings, and fire arms collection. All the very that the human hands, minds, and spirit have created. I am to be a part of this one-day, I thought; then said a small silent prayer that I repeat daily "Thank you for my life. Thank you for my wife, let me be a credit to you" As I approached the Buffalo Bill Historical Center looking to find Mr. Herbert Houze

He was off on business, somewhere back east and would be gone for several weeks. I had to put on hold my plans to become involved with the museum. We settled down to the task of making money. I asked around where I could set up my tools and work the tourist trade, engraving initials, doing portrait sketches, selling prints and so forth. I knew many people from previous exhibitions I had attended.

One of them advised me to, "Swap your slacks, tie and jacket for blue jeans, boots and a cowboy hat, then go see a man named Bob Edgar."

Bob and Terry Edgar were the owners of "Old Trail Town," an assemblage of buildings dating from the past century. He and his wife and family had scoured the area finding historical wood buildings, carefully dismantling them, then hauling them with huge effort back to Cody and reassembled them on a large parcel of land nearby. They were both interesting and hospitable to me. Bob gave me a space to work in one of his buildings, where I engraved a Colt Single Action revolver for him. I also picked up several small commissions from businesspersons of the area.

Steel print plate, "Old Trail Town" portraiture.

Franca found work cleaning motel rooms; also, she supplied one of the many restaurants in Cody with baked lasagna. She would have that little gas stove going full blast all evening making her pastas in the sweltering summer heat. I would take the garden hose and sprinkle the black tar roof of the tiny apartment, trying to bring the temperatures down to a tolerable level.

We made money as best we could. In the course of talking to the interested tourists who stopped to look at my work, several suggested that I go to Florida and work there.

"Surely you would make a lot of money in West Palm Beach," they advised.

There were many activities going on during the summer months in Cody, gun shows, festivals, fairs, art shows etc.

I decided to exhibit at the Park County Fair in Powell.

My journal: July 30

Knife: blue ribbon. Sculpted seagull in bronze: blue ribbon. Model 1881 Marlin, engraved, blue ribbon, print plate called 'Memories': blue ribbon. Print plate called 'Predator': blue ribbon. I entered seven items; and received five blue ribbons awards.

I was proud of this effort, but blue ribbons do not put gas in a car nor do they pay rent. When the winds touched by Jack Frost began to blow down the Stinking River Canyon starting in September, they brought with them the recollections of Joseph Oregon's winter. Both towns were about the same altitude. Winter was close by.

I told Franca, "We're headed south babe, we stay here we will starve"

September 12, 1985 (From my journal)
West Palm Beach Florida. Here I am in a place I do not understand, slightly confused and definitely not at home. The potential to make good sums of money seems to be here, how to open the doors is a mystery. Hot, humid, existing on air conditioning. Excuse me Lord for being such a poor servant. Tiger is unhappy. Franca is 36 today and home sick for her family.

It was only a few weeks after our arrival that Tiger became sick. We took him to a veterinarian for an exam. He had contracted feline leukemia and we put him to sleep. We held each other and cried as the vet administered the shot.

October 17th: Goodbye to Tiger.
You were a friend to Franca and me, the best pal we had in America, we adventurous three. I'm glad I caught you a fish and petted you. I'm glad I loved you. Your memory will always make me smile. I will see you again someday.

In Florida, I worked exclusively at Billy Bob's shop in Pompano Beach. There I engraved daily, finishing several fine weapons

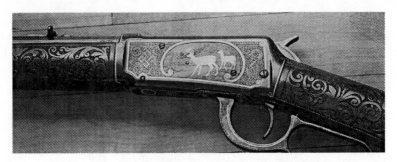

Model 1894 Winchester, woodcarving, engraving.

Franca soon found employment as caretaker of a family's eight-year-old son and their home. They, like so many others, developed a deep attachment to Franca. After three months, we had made enough money to afford to return to Italy. The Parente family was close to tears when we departed, especially their son Josh, who loved Franca.

Italy had been the grandest adventure and I had many friends among the engravers there. The United States, as far as I was concerned, had changed. I saw things in a different light. I had become dissatisfied with people's attitudes, always too busy. I started to resent the intense bombardment of media, with all their blather that was not worth the time to read or listen to.

"Yep, folks, the computers are going to fail in the year 2000," they, the media, would yell.

"Run! The sky is falling" and 80% of the nation starts running to hide like dumb little chickens.

Living in Italy had been great. There was thirty minutes of news at 9 p.m., followed by the Simpson's unless there was a soccer match. I found that to be just right. People were affectionate, gifted artisans, well dressed and happy. There were no junk cars strewn around. Saw little that I found disturbing to my peace of mind. I loved Italy, but had to prove myself as an engraver in the United States. Franca agreed that Florida was not the place for us.

She had left her family behind to follow me. A man with hopes and no last name, a man with so many chains of self-guilt wrapped around his neck that he could hardly walk. Franca's love and counsel had cut them away one by one. I knew she was homesick and needed to be with her family. We had the money, I could work anywhere in the world. I had no boss, no overhead, just a small bag of chisels and engraving hammer. All I needed to make a few dollars was a pencil and a piece of paper.

Once again, we sold all of our accumulations, reduced our life down to three suitcases and one art box containing my tools and two ounces of pure gold for inlaying.

December 18, 1985, Franca booked our tickets. We found a neighbor who bought the reliable Plymouth Horizon.

Sold my rifle to the owner of Billy Bob's then squared myself with the bank in Walalla County. Free of all obligations, Joseph and wife set sail once more for the land of art and culture; more training for me and time for Franca to enjoy her loved ones that she misses so …

Upon our arrival in Gardone Italy., there was a continuous stream of excited friends visiting us as we settled back into Franca's small but comfortable apartment. The next six months flew by. I returned to the maestro's workshop. He set up a small space, where I took up the study of medallion making, fine gold line inlay work, also further studies of banknote engraving, filled the hours at Renato's Bottega di Incisione.

Henry rifle (reproduction), author's design

Once again, we were running low on cash. Soon I had to return to the States and really go to work.

With finished engraving showing much more mastery of my tools, I was sure I could live wherever I wished—any city, L.A., Broken Leg, Missouri—it mattered not. I was confident of success. My studies were over and I was ready to settle down. So was Franca.

"Where are we going to live?" She asked after I told her that I had to go back.

"I wasn't sure," I answered.

We talked things over, finally deciding that she would remain behind and wait for me to settle, somewhere, anywhere, and then send for her.

With one sister driving and the other one sitting in the back seat saying, "I told you so,"

We headed for the Malpensa Airport in Milan, Italy. I was laden with so much weight I could hardly make it up the iron staircase to the check-in. I was carrying back to the States all of my tools, engraving vise, presents from friends, books, sheets, pillowcases, two suitcases full of stuff plus a carry-on bag in which vise and tools were held. (I can't do that anymore.)

I remember standing on the stairwell, stopping to blow a kiss at Franca, us both with eyes brimming when the strap of the carrying case broke, leaving me to manage it and the two suitcases up the stairs to check in.

June 28th, 1985: Malpensa Airport
Franca and I are separated for the first time in quite a while. I almost cried when we said goodbye. Never the less there was inside of me a voice that says 'Go Joseph, you can make it. The end results of your labors will make your life much more beautiful.' Franca's mom said to me as she kissed me, "Goodbye, Go peacefully. Go to work."

(Later whenever Franca talked with her mother on the telephone the first thing she would ask, "And Joseph, is he working?" She would laugh and reply, "Si, mama.")

Upon arrival at Logan International Airport in Boston I collected my bags, fixed the broken carry-on strap, called custom to see if the pistol I had engraved while working for Maestro Renato Sanzogni had cleared. It would not clear until the following week. Satisfied that it had at least gotten back to the United States, I caught a Greyhound bus headed back to New Hampshire, home of my stepfather and mother. What a strange feeling that was.

"All aboard for Lowell, Nashua, Manchester, and Concord."

I felt my present and past collide into a storm of mixed emotions as I stored bags then got on board the bus.

The green Hudson cab stopped across the street from my mother's house. I started wondering if it was perhaps better if I got a hotel room or contact Uncle Waldo, mother's youngest and only brother. I sighed, paid the driver, and collected my ton of luggage, waited for the traffic to clear on the busy four-lane highway, remembering when it once had been a dirt road. The house looked lovingly cared for. It was white with green trim, driveway clean, and asphalted with a neat well-maintained garage on one side. Ernest always was a neat and tidy man. I did no longer hate him, I understood him. I had come to terms with it all, and forgave him. He was doing what he thought was right, as simple as that.

He was polishing the chrome on a new Buick Riviera. He paused to watch me cross the road. I was halfway up the drive before he realized who I was.

"Well for Christ's sakes—Joe. What are you doing here?" Without waiting for an answer, he called for my mother, who was in the kitchen. "Hey Lil, guess who's here, Joe's here."

"Hi Dad," is all I had time to say. Mother came out on the sun porch, looked at me then said.

"Joey, oh my Joey, It's you." I was quickly at her side and I hugged her.

"Hi, mother I'm glad to see you."

She returned my hug and gave me a dry peck on the cheek. I no longer felt any bitterness towards her. I could understand her. She gave me all the love that she had; it's just that I needed more. No one's fault, that's the way things were.

Over tea and cookies, I explained my appearance.

"How did you get here?" "Where's Franca?" I explained.

"Are you separated?" I explained.

With each explanation, I could sense the warmth of my welcome diminishing. Finally, we came to the details.

"I need a place to stay and get organized. Just for a few days until I find a car, wait for my artwork to arrive and clear from customs, then I will be on the way."

A fog-like silence filled the sunlit kitchen.

Mother said. "Well, Joe. We were just getting ready to go up to our camp. We're building a new home up there and we won't be back for a week."

"That's O K," I assured them.

"Well Joe, we always shut the hot water off when we go."

"That's not a problem mother; I have had many cold baths. I don't mind a bit."

"Well, I guess it's all right. What do you think Ernest?"

"It's O K with me. Just make sure you lock the door when you're gone."

My accommodations settled. I waved 'bye-bye' as they left for their lakeside camp an hour later.

The first thing needed was wheels. I had a big road trip ahead of me. I contacted Uncle Waldo, he more than willingly offered to chauffer me around, even take me back to Boston when the dueling pistol cleared the U.S. Duty House. I had $1,000 dollars worth of German Marks plus a couple of hundred US currencies in my possession.

My first exhibition took place on July 12 in Cody, Wyoming 2800 miles west of Boston. Then, after Cody, I had to return to the East Coast for a meeting with several of the firearms manufacturers in Connecticut. I was hoping to establish a working relationship with the new Parker Gun Company and the Fox Gun Company. Then after leaving Connecticut, I'd go south, back to Florida, to settle some unfinished business with Billy Bob's, then exhibit at the West Palm Beach gun show. After Florida, I planned to go to Houston, for the Texas Gun Collector's Show. From Houston, up to the Broadmoor Hotel in Colorado Springs,

Colorado for another exhibition and from there back to Cody, Wyoming. Then find a suitable home for Franca and me, finally settle down and start making money.

To make this trip I needed a good dependable car, I had been looking at used cars and had found nothing dependable for $1000. At the Chrysler-Plymouth dealership, I found a brand new Omni exactly like the one I had sold in Florida, same color. "Yes, the salesman said, this car could definitely be purchased for a $1000 down payment, upon proof of employment, home address, and credit card of course."

By some miracle, I got qualified, primarily because of Winchester letters of recommendation. Said I lived with my mother and Ernest. I then contacted Ernest's insurance agent, told him I was the long lost son and needed coverage on the new 1987 Plymouth Horizon, using the bank in Joseph Oregon as credit reference. Only in America, can a man get off an airplane, not have a job, nor a credit card or last name, and buy a new car.

July 3rd, 1986: New Hampshire
Finally have a car to start my trip. Have had to strip my finances down to the bottom, $40 left and I have to be in Cody next Thursday. Looks like I'll have to become a hustler and a schemer. However, I am not worried, just nervous. Life as an artist sure is different. Looks like I have to be Gypsy Joe for a while. Talked to my Franca today, sure miss her. Please, keep an eye on me.

I said goodbye to my uncle Waldo, thanked him for his help and headed for Wyoming. As I drove, I started to think of ways to get money. Portraits would pick up a few dollars, but I was in a hurry, a man on a mission. I needed someone to share expenses. It was outside of Chicago when I seized my opportunity.

Standing at the truck stop parking lot where I was refueling, three young men in their twenties, all with backpacks, one with a mandolin, each dressed in lederhosen, hiking boots, wool socks and all sunburned to the point where they looked like French fries. I parked, walked over, and asked if they wanted a ride. It turned out they were hoping to see the Western United States. An agreement was quickly made, they pay gas, food, help with the driving and I would deliver them to the East Gate of Yellowstone park in Wyoming. Twenty-four hours later, I dropped them off in Cody. Some days the sun shines a bit brighter than others do.

I set up my tools and worked at the Winchester Collectors gun show for its duration, busily engraving, making some much-needed money, the sharp clicking of the hammer drew crowds of people to watch me work. There I picked up a commission from Freedom Arms, along with promises of additional work. Loaded my tools in the trunk of the Horizon, headed east.

July 15th, 1986, Cody, Wyoming, Gun Show is over. I have had some success. Now have post office box, auto insurance, business cards, business address, and $800 in cash to start the rest of this trip. I wish I had a good solid plan but I don't, just dreams.

Chapter eighteen

"SCULPTING"

By the end of September, I had found a nice clean small house with a tool shed converted into a reasonably warm studio. I had earned enough money to get Franca and the new cat, Tigretta, back to Cody, Wyoming. My commission work was steadily increasing. Still it was not enough to stop me from exhibiting and traveling.

From my diary:
Off to Denver, roundtrip by air, $75 in my pocket, carrying an assortment of guns, knives, pistols, and revolvers, strange things for a man of peace.
December 25th, 1986 Christmas Day, Cody Wyoming, The sun shines in my studio. There is a pine wreath upon the door. By my drawing table sits a new stool. My heart is clear, my love is true, for all things I want to say, I thank you. Today Franca and I went hiking in the mountains, full of energy and love. Well thank you dear Force somewhere out in space. I don't believe many are as blessed as we, Franca, Tigretta, and me. Let me be a credit to this human race.

It was while working at the tool shed studio I started engraving my own designs. I was determined to gain credit from the B.B.H.C. for my skills. I found a model 94 Winchester that was suitable. Bought it for $195 Dollars, $75 down and the balance in 30 days. From my journal:

May 9th, 1987
This week I sold my first rifle to the B.B.H.C., $2,450 for five years of learning. I may not remember one tenth of the people I have met in my lifetime, but I can remember all the details of my engravings.

On one side of that rifle, I put portraits of Chief Sitting Bull and WF Cody. I left a blank inscription panel.

I reassembled the rifle and brought the walnut stock to the best luster; put it in a box and took it to the museum, then made an appointment to see Mr. Houze. I showed him the rifle and asked him if he would purchase it for the money I asked. The work had taken two weeks to complete so I set the price at $200 a day. "Charge what you need," one fellow engraver had told me while we were talking shop.

I left the rifle with the curator, giving him time for careful examination of my portraiture under a jewelry loupe. He called the next day and said "yes," they would buy the rifle.

"Fine," I said …, [recalling Christies auction] "But I want to be paid first and then I will cut the inscription in the blank panel."

They issued me a check and I cut the words 'Buffalo Bill Historical Center.'

Model 94 Winchester carbine, (B.B.H.C)

With my career now on solid foundation and the workload up to 40 or 50 hours, which was all the work I could handle. It was now time to collect for all those unpaid and underpaid hours I had stood in front of a vise. I began raising my prices. Generally, clients would come to me with their own ideas for a design and, of course, want an estimate of cost. If it was meticulously detailed work, I knew approximately how long it would take. My rule of thumb, so to speak, was what I could cover with my thumb took about six to eight hours, six days to finish one side, six for the other and two for the miscellaneous. Some days I would work ten, twelve hours until stressed, then I might take three, or four days off and go fishing or play poker.

To be financially successful, an engraver must be two things; He must be fast and he must be very good. People would be amazed in answer to a question of "How long did it take to engrave that?" I would say, "One hour."

I arranged with the manager of the museum gift shop [at that time, Ev Diehl,] to engrave his series of .22 rifles, fifteen in all, with the same vignette of a man holding a rifle out to a boy sitting on a log with a spotted dog by the boy's side. The entire edition sold out in a very short time.

With Franca working as a waitress, we soon had enough money to move into a comfortable home with a whole number for an address. I built an 11x14 moveable building as a studio. From my journal:

August 4th, 1987
My little studio is almost complete. With windows facing north and a beautiful view of the street. A pointed shake roof and timbers rot proof, my little studio will last me all my life. To be at home with my love, my work and my cat let me be content only with that.

I believed we would stay put and never move again. I thought I had fulfilled most of my dreams and goals, now it was Franca's turn.

It began with a chance meeting, a couple from the Chicago area. They were in Cody for a large auction of Indian items. During their visit, they came across the display of my work. The man was short, about my height, slim, well dressed and all business in his manner. The woman was so striking that I found it difficult not to stare at her. Beautiful women make me nervous.

"Hello," she said. "What a talented man. Your work is beautiful. Have you ever considered sculpting?" She asked. I was accustomed to people's appreciation of my work but was still a bit embarrassed when complimented.

"Thank you very much," I answered. "But there's always room for improvement." Moreover, no, I was not interested in sculpting which allowed much for error where as engraving was so demanding that no mistakes were permissible. I ended by saying "I could do things that few sculptors could do." She thanked me. They continued down the aisle looking over the wares of other exhibitors, a short time late the woman returned, this time by herself. She asked me about myself, my training, etcetera … I told her that I had trained in Italy and had pieces of work in the permanent collection of the Buffalo Bill Historical Center.

When I finished she said, "That's exactly why I think you would make a fine sculptor. Could you sculpt a western horse and rider?"

I said, I "believed if I put my mind to it, I could."

How long did I think it would take? The beautiful woman wanted to know.

My longest engraving project had taken three months to complete. I could not imagine a clay horse and man twelve inches tall could take any longer, so I said, "About three months."

"I'll be in touch," she said taking one of my business cards and departing. After the show, I discussed the meeting with Franca and then put it out of my mind. Two weeks later, I received a twenty-dollar check and a copy of Harry Jackson's book on lost wax casting, along with a note explaining that the money was to buy sculpting materials.

"I guess they are seriously thinking about me doing a bronze," I said to Franca.

Twenty dollars was not enough money to make me stop engraving … I deposited the check, read Harry's book and went on with my usual business. In November, I received a call from Mrs. Davies. They were holding an auction in Scottsdale, Arizona. She asked if I would like to come down and see their operation. They offered to take care of my expenses and travel. I accepted but opted to drive at my own expense rather than fly. I was not sure I wanted to sculpt and did not want to become obligated.

In November, I once again took to the road. I arrived in Scottsdale early the next morning, having driven straight through, stopping for gas, and then making a small pot of espresso coffee. Three cups of espresso coffee, fifteen minutes of rest and I could drive another six hours non-stop. Relying on habits I had learned while traveling those many thousands of miles across the United States, sometimes carrying as much as $150,000 in engraved weapons plus cash, I always carefully checked out my destination for security and safety. I cruised around Scottsdale looking for the building where the auction was to be held. As I drove, I could not help but think to myself that the same architects that had designed West Palm Beach shopping malls also worked in Scottsdale. I located the building, checked it and the surrounding neighborhood to see if the streets were clear and free of broken glass. The residences looked prosperous, no bars on the windows and doors, everything looked good, I parked where I could observe things and doze.

At 7 A.M., the first unloading crew arrived, raised the building's roll up door, and unlocked the two semi-trailers.

I wandered over to watch the workers unload. When I saw the treasures that the loading crews were carrying down the loading ramp and into the building, I was amazed. I could not believe the quantity and quality of the items that were there. Persian rugs piled two feet high, fur coats by the rack, original oil paintings, beautiful lamps, china, crystal, flatware, and boxes of linens. Antique autos began to arrive in the parking lot, a Bentley, a red Ferrari, two Mercedes.

Photo of the artist

Then the boxes and cartons of unopened treasures, Mrs. Davies, and her auctioneer partner drove up in a white El Dorado. Soon, all were setting up previewing tables, opening cartons. I felt like a kid at Christmas. Everyone was working to the directions of the auctioneer. His name was Joe and he made up for his short stature by being loud and rough talking.

I really did not like the first impressions of him. Mrs. Davies on the other hand was quite kind and polite. She offered me coffee while explaining about the activity. The auction was set for 2:00 P.M. on Sunday and they would be working long hours to get things set up. Two tractor-trailers full of things to be unloaded, waxed, polished, and set up in groupings. If I wished, I could work with them and she would pay for my labor. There would not be much time for discussion until Sunday evening. It was fine with me; I set to work unpacking boxes. It was when setting up a table with fine English china that the idea smacked me, like a bolt out of the blue. Everything needed to start a small exclusive restaurant was right here: tables, linens, silver, everything.

When the auction was over, I was both impressed and pooped. I stayed with the work crew in a rented townhouse; Sunday night was beer, burgers and a swimming pool.

I slept soundly for a good ten hours. Refreshed, I joined Mrs. Davies and Joe at breakfast. They talked about the proposed sculpture over coffee, its cost, what profits it would bring and how to split them, marketing, and other business details. Finally, I had to decide what direction I was going. I liked the talk, and the money was attractive. It was then that I asked if I could make some kind of a trade for the furnishings of a small restaurant. Then explained how Franca had always wanted one, and that they had access to all that was necessary. After more consideration, they agreed that once the sculpture was in bronze and the molds ready for production, they would make arrangements.

Based on all these factors, I made the commitment, signed the contract, and headed north towards home and Franca, bringing her a pair of beautiful Capo di Monte lamps and a nice wrought iron and walnut entry table. Later after kisses and coffee, I told Franca that I had taken the commission.

I put all engraving projects aside to begin the research necessary to do the sculpting at once. It did not take me long to realize that I had gotten once again into an interesting predicament. I had no idea what sculpting was about. I knew little about the human body, never mind the horse. Drawing it is one thing. Sculpting in the round is another. This project was in a whole other league. I started the commission by borrowing all the library books I could find on the subject of humans, horses, saddles, bridles and bits. Then spent days trying to understand the skeletal structures of both figures. I entered into a new world of learning. I was excited and very happy.

The first problem I encountered was that of design. I was going to do this work; and wanted to do it well, as it was going to have my name on it. The training as an engraver makes me see details. I was terrified at the thought that more experience people could criticize my new work to the point of embarrassment. I made every effort to make sure that the wax model was as perfect as it could possibly be.

How was I going to create the illusion that a solid mass of metal might conceivably move? I decided that the most dynamic geometric form was rhombic. Working on that premise, then sculpted the horse and rider with those boundaries. The most difficult part was to give the rider a reason, galloping to the rescue of his cattle herd perhaps. I tried a pistol as a point of first interest. What was the point?

Every sculptor of the West has used that trick. I finally made up my mind that the horse was to be the focal beginning. Once sure, of the objectives, I began work.

It was in March that I went to the foundry to pick up the final molds for the first casting of what I had entitled, 'Winchester's Time.'

I labored on the wax model, once satisfied, I took it to the local saddle shop to see the owner. He was a man who had bought, sold, rode, and traded more horses than anyone I knew. He was sitting next to his workbench half asleep when I entered his well-equipped shop. The tinkling bell woke him; I introduced myself, than asked him to do me the favor of looking at the wax model and giving me his experienced opinion. He took it from me, looked it over at arms length, turned it all-ways, and then said, "When I was a young man, this is the horse I loved to ride." I wanted to kiss the guy; instead, I retrieved the model, shook his hand, thanked him, and went to the local foundry to have it cast in bronze. The sculpting process had been very difficult, the casting a near disaster. The final bronze was pitted and somewhat distorted from the foundry. I took it to my studio, got out engraving punches and chisels, and chased the entire piece out with hammers. When I could go no farther, I took the bronze to my admired friend and sculptor, Harry Jackson. I found him at his desk and we greeted each other in the Italian way with a warm embrace. After I had pulled up a chair and we had settled, I removed the bronze from its protective cloth and handed it to Harry, saying, "I've finished this little bronze and I'd like you to have a look at it."

"If you wanted me to look at it why didn't you bring the wax model, not the finished piece?"

"I didn't want to bother you Harry, this is my work," I replied.

Harry grunted, picked up the bronze, and began to study it intently and seriously. He sat for a long time, saying nothing, just looking at my work, scowling and clucking.

I reached the point of such concern that I finally asked, "Is it that bad Harry?" He responded, "Considering you know nothing of sculpting, horses, or anatomy, it's a hell of a piece. It has movement, balance, and life. I'm in awe of what you have accomplished."

"From you Harry, I consider that to be a great compliment." shook his hand and said, "You're a hell of an artist Harry."

He answered. "It takes one to know one."

I then left him to his life's labor.

Finally satisfied, I booked the flight to Chicago and delivered the bronze for approval. Mrs. Davies was thrilled with the piece. Joe, the auctioneer was more interested to see if I had put testicles on the horse.

"Great!" He said as he held the horse upside down.

"You put balls on it, that's excellent, I just love it. It will sell."

"WINCHESTER'S TIME", Bronze sculpture

Well satisfied with the results of my labor, they approved the first consignment of furniture. It was the beginnings of Franca's restaurant. Happy, I returned home to tell Franca the news.

Shortly there after, my mother and Ernest visited us. They had driven out west towing behind their new car a camping trailer in which to spend their nights on the road. We were all sitting on a small front porch enjoying the shade of the large spruce tree that grew there. I said to my mother, "You know, mother, I'm sure glad you did not have an abortion when you became pregnant with me."

"Well, we didn't know about those sorts of things back then," she replied.

May 8th, 1988

Today is mother's day. Thanks mom. If it weren't for you no pen would write, no voice would laugh, and no mind would whir, no tongue would taste the wine. No heart would feel this love divine.

Chapter nineteen

"FRANCA'S LITTLE RESTAURANT"

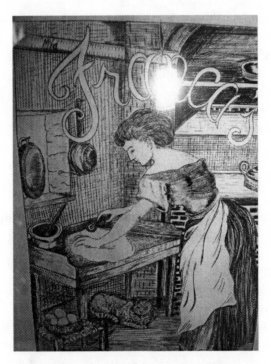

Steel plate engraving for Franca's restaurant.

With assurance that the needed furnishings were being set aside for Franca's restaurant, we started searching for a suitable location. We finally decided on a very large old home just off the main street of Sheridan Avenue. It was not in good shape but it would do, and it was affordable. We arranged a lease, and then started preparing for our next adventure in this uncertain soup we call life.

Taking sheets of newspaper, we placed them about the two large rooms on the main floor determining where tables and chairs would go. We bought a large stainless steel, three-compartment sink for washing dishes, found a Plummer to install it, a four-burner double oven domestic stove from Sears. I cleaned and re-seeded the front lawn, repaired the locks and gates got the place painted a neutral blue trimmed in ivory .Giving truth to the adage. A coat of paint can hide a multitude of sins. Then while taking a break planted an herb garden, had the studio moved to its new location in the backyard and once again went back to work, I was working without a view, without a vista to rest my eyes upon while taking a break from staring into a ten-power jeweler's loupe for hours.

My view looking north was the kitchen window with as big, cheap, second hand air-conditioner as I could stuff into it, Franca's geraniums, a few scraggly trees, and the corner of city hall parking lot. To the south, the alley that served the business community with its usual Main street restaurants, bars, t-shirt shops, art galleries, hotels, motels. The noisy alley had as much traffic, if not more, than the main Sheridan Avenue.

The view of the east was the back of a large, ugly, yellow tin and block building. To the west, I was looking through the broken slats of the fences, at the trash thrown there by the clients of the Silver Dollar bar. I had to be content with being able to see Franca working in her kitchen and smell the aromas that came from her kitchen.

Even though setting up the restaurant was a tremendous amount of work, I was very glad that I had been able to give Franca her restaurant.

May 21ˢᵗ, 1989: Rockton, Illinois
More gifts, Gifts in abundance. I have received so many that I need a twenty-five foot truck to carry them all back to Cody. English china, pots and pans, antique furnishings from across many lands. Lamps, curtains, and things of Irish lace are going to put a smile on my loved one's face. Franca's restaurant next week will be a reality. A place to dine, a beautiful place, I have made friends with nice people and because of it; my wife's little dream is going to become a reality. The furnishings are loaded and ready to come back to Wyoming. In ten days, the restaurant will be open. I am sure it will be the talk of the town.

The Trip Back to Cody (From my journal)

I have driven 400 miles. It is now 2 a.m. and I am sitting in line with other truckers. A violent thunderstorm rocking us, rain is beating upon the roof with vio-

lence of a waterfall; the air is full of blistering light. I want to write this as I take advantage of the pause in driving. 1600 miles in this gutless beast, that says 'Ryder Rents.'

I had the most unnerving experience at about 1 a.m. I was struggling along at 55 m p h., as fast as the truck would go when a huge tractor-trailer rig roared past me, damn near taking off my driver's side mirror. It pulled in front of me with inches to spare, and then slowed down until all I could see was the rear end of the trailer. Suddenly another rig pulled up parallel to my hood and another pulled in behind, placing me in a box with no room to maneuver. They kept me in that formation for a good ten minutes. All I could do was steer straight, keep my speed, and pray that the brake lights in the front tractor rig did not go on. The weather started getting hairy, so they quit their game and roared off on the interstate out of sight.

Finally, the trip came to its exhausting end. After a bit of rest, we began unpacking and putting in order the dining room areas. Over the cracked and nail-filled plaster walls, I hung the artwork. Oils, watercolors, intaglio prints, pastels, mezzotints,—art of every imaginable technique, Beautiful, beautiful colorful art. The tables were set with white damask linens, cut crystal goblets. Ruby and jade colored water glasses, fine wine glasses, flowers fresh for every table, fine china from England, Bavaria, and Italy made each place setting a feast for the eyes. Help was hired.

Finally, I was able to say. "Franca my love, Here is your little restaurant. It is yours, not mine. I do not want to be the waiter, host, or busboy. I want to return to my studio and continue working."

As anyone who has eaten at Franca's over the following ten years or so can tell you, that did not work out very well. She was busy and I was available. I became busboy, waiter, dishwasher, table setter, general handy man, grounds keeper, defender of my wife's dreams. The first defense of Franca's dreams happened on July 4 weekend, 1989.

It was Friday, the busiest night of our restaurant. It was hot and I was tired. I had finally been able to retreat to my studio. I had been working for about a half hour, long enough for my nerves and fingers to steady. I was inlaying gold into a Colt revolver for the Wyoming's Centennial. I wanted the gold work to be the finest and most intricate, most delicate I could execute.

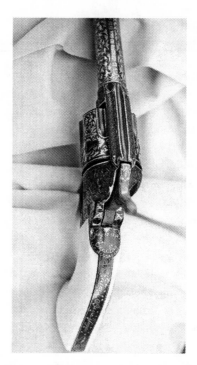

Top view Colt single action, Wyoming Centennial

I had been working just long enough that I achieved total concentration when a deafening vibration penetrated the quiet. Losing concentration, I put my tools down, got down from the stool, and went outside to see what the racket was.

The sound was coming from a sand-covered lot where a volleyball court had been set up, part of the Silver Dollar bar and grill—the "Dollar" we called it. The Dollar had a reputation for fistfights, knife fights and even gun fights in its past. However, they served cold beer and good hamburgers. It was very popular place for the young crowd and bikers.

Franca also came outside to see what the din was about. We met in the back-yard.

"What is it? What can be making that horrible sound?" she had to yell

It was so loud I could hardly hear what she was saying. It was close to 2 p.m. and in four hours; we would be opening for business.

"Let's go see what's going on," I suggested. We walked hand-in-hand the quarter of a block to the Dollar. We were speechless when we saw a heavy metal rock band testing the huge truck-sized speakers, amplifiers, electric cables, and their instruments.

We walked up to the nice looking young man with his hair frizzed and bleached blond. I introduced Franca and myself, explained that our business was next door and that evening, we would appreciate it if they would turn the volume down. He looked at me as if I were speaking a different language and said, "Fuck you."

I simply replied, "At 6 p.m. turn it down or I will do something about it." We returned to our house. I was starting to get very annoyed. The more I thought about his reply, the madder I got. Then the band broke loose with full bass volume. Franca came back into the yard and we looked at each other.

"You have to do something!" She cried.

That was it. I got on the phone, called the mayor, then the police. No one would move against the Dollar. The city council had given them a variance to play music and sell beer for the next 24 hours. When the police sergeant told me this, I took matters into my own hands. First, I called the mayor again and asked him if he could do something about it. He again told me no. Then I called back to the police station, asked them if they could do something else about it. They said no. In my studio, I had a full sized axe with a short stubby wooden handle, purchased at a garage sale for a dollar or two.

As the reservation time of our guests drew near, Franca became more desperate. Her dinner was about to be ruined by a bunch of thoughtless jerks. I slipped the axe under my belt, put a sport coat over it, and then walked casually over to the Silver Dollar Bar and Grill. I entered into the crowd of partiers, searching for the umbilical cord to the machine from hell. I was over dressed and stood out like a sore thumb.

Suddenly, I saw it twisting its way across the concrete floor. I knew wood was a poor conductor of electricity. I was concerned that someone would see me skulking through the crowd and hear a woman screaming, "There's a man with an axe! There's a man with an axe!" If that had happened, I was going to end up looking like hamburger by the time they got through with me.

Fortunately, nobody paid attention, until the sparks flew and the band fell into a silent twanging of electric guitars without amplification. Hands grabbed my wrists yanking the axe away, for a brief moment; I thought some one was going to brain me. I was pinned to the wall by half dozen men. The owner was staring me in the eyeballs, fist raised, screaming. "You fucking crazy son of a bitch."

When I get really pissed off, I don't back away. I have a very angry person who resides in me that comes forth, he is restrained, but under great duress, I cannot hold him back. Ready to fight to the finish, I snarled right back at his ugly face, spit my words at him wishing they were bullets "And your Dammed music drove me there. Go ahead, hit me you asshole and I'll own this fucking place."

We came to a Mexican standoff. To Franca's relief the police, two cars full of them, came. They put me in handcuffs and into their custody. Thus, it was that the front page of the Cody Enterprise headlines read, "Man with Axe Silences Dollar Bar." The results of this rash action had surprising endings. People began eating at Franca's just to say how much they appreciated us. The judge, in whose court I later had to appear on destruction of property charges, dismissed me with a minimum payment of $20 court cost.

"I live two miles out of town," he said. "And I could hear it myself. By the way, what is this thing with your name?"

I explained to him that it was my full legal name.

"How do you plead? 'Defiantly guilty your honor" I responded.

"Case dismissed!" he said.

The owner of the Dollar bar's competition, the Down Towner bar, asked if I would sell him the axe, after the Police would release it from the evidence room. I said, "No."

Then he offered me $100 for it. I quickly changed my mind, and engraved the axe head with the words, "No guts, No peace," and took the $100 bill.

The restaurant took care and attention to grow, the first two years were tenuous at best. Though the place was open to high praise, the locals tended to prefer steak, baked potatoes, green beans, and garlic toast; it took time before they tried baked leg of veal stuffed with prunes in a cognac sauce, leek fritters, beets and green pea soup, arugula salad and Focaccia bread. Nevertheless, slowly the monthly income under Franca's guidance began to increase.

It was but two years later that the restaurant became self-sufficient. Soon there was enough cash to buy the guns I preferred to engrave. I thought of them as canvases and those canvases of steel cost between $800 and $8000. There is some quality in the antique Winchesters that I found instantly appealing. I would wander the guns shows looking at the several thousands of guns on display. Somewhere on one of those tables, I would find a neglected treasure, buy it, take it back to the studio, and disassemble it. While I was handling the frame (that's the part to engrave) my mind would contemplate, "Who owned this?" and "What events in history might it have been present to be a part of"

After some research, I would eventually come up with a theme. From that came the character of the work. The rest came through more reading and research. For example, I bought a Winchester model 1892 carbine at a gun show. Who would have used such a rifle at that time in history? Perhaps a miner had struck it rich in Alaska. Now I had the character of the rifle, and decided to engrave it with a mining theme.

I would then research the theme at the library looking for the right photos, drawings, etcetera, so that I could produce accurate engravings. I learned early on, that it was easy to overprice a piece of work. I was trying to maintain $50 an hour rate, but if I got involved in a very complex piece of work, could easily price myself out of the market. No matter how beautiful those rifles might have been, they were difficult to digest, even with Franca's cognac and prune sauce.

The collector's were paying top dollar for premium grade, factory engraved guns. Many of them sell for $500,000 and up. As a contemporary engraver replicating these old masterpieces, I could easily charge 10 to 20 percent of the value and find a good market.

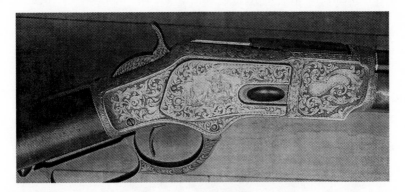

Model 1873 Winchester, inspired by engraver L. D. Nimschke, circa 1865

One bright and windy day, Franca and I were walking to Stecks I.G.A. Grocers to buy the necessities for that night's dinner reservations. There was a wonderful old French country style, two-story stucco house located on the other side of the Avenue

"Wouldn't that be a wonderful place to put the restaurant?" Franca would always say as we passed by. I agreed, yes it would.

One day on the way to the store, stuck in the still brown, half-frozen lawn, was a realtor's "for sale" sign. Without changing stride, I cut across the street, up the sidewalk to the house of 1421 Rumsey Avenue. The door to the antique shop located there was open. I went in, found the owner, and asked directly, how much the price was. She told me. Then I asked, "Would you consider selling on a contract?" No bank was going to finance Franca and me at that point of our lives, I knew that for sure.

"Would $10,000 down and $800 per month buy this house?" I asked.

"Yes, it would," Mrs. Smith, replied.

I asked permission to look around a bit. Having built houses in a past live I knew exactly what to look for. After a good examination I decided that I could make the place beautiful, first I would have to strip the entire lower level down to bare studs and rafters. It would be a lot of work but I was sure that we could do it. The house had many wonderful features: maple floors, charming fireplace, and entry, space for a large efficient kitchen and a comfortable space for dining.

I made an instant decision, "Mrs. Smith, we will buy it. We do not have $10,000 right now, but I will be back in ten days with the money. If some one else comes along between now and then it wasn't meant to be" On my return home I told Franca the news.

Ever practical, she asked, "Where will we get the money?" "I'll sell the Colt pistol and a couple of lesser pieces," I said.

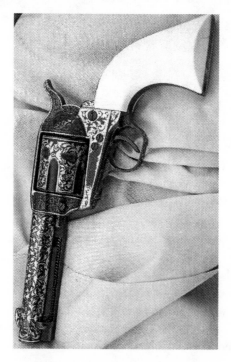

Colt single action, gold and ivory work.

The Wyoming centennial pistol and the gold work in it was my greatest effort, the steel quite hard and difficult to undercut. The work was extremely fine and the design quite delicate. I had hopes of selling it to the Buffalo Bill Historical Center or to a private Wyoming collector. I had carved a set of ivory stocks for it and inlaid them in steel and gold. It had drawn the highest praise at the Gun Makers and Engraver's Guild Show in Las Vegas. Mr. Houze examined the work then wrote a letter, stating that the gold work was as good as any he had ever seen.

Again, I contacted Mrs. Davies and asked if they were soon to have an auction. Yes, one was coming up in Santa Fe, New Mexico next week. I faxed her copy of the museum letter and photos so that the auction's brochure could advertise the Colt revolver, loaded up the Plymouth and headed south to Santa Fe. The revolver sale drew a good crowd of collectors.

When it came on the block produced a very spirited bidding. It brought the hammer closing at $11,000. One other gun brought the necessary cash to make the down payment on the house. I took six months off from engraving and started remodeling. Franca continued running the restaurant while I worked daily on the new house. When all was ready, we moved everything out of one location into the other, hired a building mover who once again picked up my studio and placed it on his trailer for the short drive down the street.

Model 1886 Winchester, John Ulrich design.

All the labors were worth it. With the charm of the new location, Franca's lovingly prepared meals, and her amazing ability to manage the business, the restaurant flourished and prospered. I now had the luxury of enough cash to buy higher priced rifles for my canvases, also the time and funds needed to continue to sculpt. The average price of my engraving work increased to $10,000 and they were selling almost as fast as I could produce them.

Three years after we took possession of the house, we paid off the mortgage.

Usually the best way to discuss difficult issues is after a good meal and wine, in between tiramisu and espresso. At the right moment I said, "Franca my dear, I think now that the restaurant is successful I should take a percentage of the profit."

"Oh, how much would that be?" I took another sip of coffee, let it roll around my tongue a bit, smiled, and took her hand for I knew what her answer would be.

"I think that if I'm going to continue as host, waiter, busboy, table setter, reservation taker, floor mopper, window cleaner, and yard man, 50% sounds fair."

She thought for a minute, and then answered with the words I longed to hear "Well, I think it would be less expensive if I hire help."

"I agree with you my dear," I said, as I finished the last bit of the tiramisu. And so it was that Franca's Italian Dining lost one of its most unmanageable employees.

From my journal
March 19
Leaving for Italy, Thank you for giving me this day, Thank you for giving me my wife, Thank you for giving me my life, Ray and I are off for a gambler's dream trip. We are going to play poker in the card rooms of Europe. Tickets and auto reservations made and paid for out of poker winnings. Amsterdam, Paris, Nice, Vienna, Hungary, Czechoslovakia and then down to Italy, This time I am not hitchhiking. I am going there in a sports car. I will be taking a bronze with me. I hope to show it to some of the art galleries to see if there is a market for Wyoming art.

"FAVORITE MOMENTS" Bronze sculpture

"PARTING GLANCE" Bronze sculpture

One of the hundred reasons that I adore my wife is that she is super practical, which keeps us in balance. If it were not for her, I never would have known love and happiness. If not for me, the restaurant would never have become a reality. When Franca's opened, I thought it was going to be her hobby, something to enjoy, but not to make money. My hope was, if we broke even that would be fine. I was spending so many hours in my studio I was glad for her to have her dream, but never expected that she was dreaming of a moneymaking machine.

"With you," she would say, "I will never be bored or hungry. But with me, you will never be broke."

She was right. It was not but a short while after we opened that I sold three bronzes in one evening. It was amazingly easy to sell some nice people from Vermont a bit of my artwork, after they had feasted and consumed a good bottle of Brunello. Many times the dinner check would be $4,000-$6,000.

Model 94 rifle, bank-note work for the Buffalo Bill Historical Center

"TERRITORIAL DISPUTE" Bronze sculpture

I have always wondered when the buyers woke up next morning, looked at the bronze parked on their motel coffee table if they did not say. "Did we really buy that last night"?

For us the restaurant was a form of theatre. Each night we could go through the ritual of preparing for opening. I would scrub my fingernails trying to remove the ink, soot, and wax. Franca would take thirty-minute rest; we would shower, dress, and descend the stairs. I would make sure the walkway was clear and clean as I made my way to turn on the open sign.

There is no question in my mind that Franca's Italian Dining and the people that I met there once again altered the course of my life. I had developed many crude ideas about people. I especially disliked attorneys, medical people, and politicians, but after several years of being their host, I realized I was wrong. They were mostly all polite, intelligent, and interesting people.

I had many fond memories of Franca's and some very awkward ones as well. Some of the fondest are having Willy Nelson and his band as our guests, and when a customer got on his knees and proposed to his girlfriend. Taking the time to enjoy the last customer of the evening made us many true and good friends. People would come in to eat as strangers and at the end of the evening; they would leave us their address and telephone number inviting us to visit.

"If you're ever in Miami, Paris, New York, London, please come visit."

I enjoyed overhearing comments about the artwork that I had prominently displayed throughout the dining rooms, especially regarding my bronzes.

"Is that a Russell or a Remington?" someone would ask looking at one of my bronzes.

"No, that's my work," I would reply as I filled their water glasses and set the wine list on the table.

I enjoyed the look of amazement on their faces as they exclaimed in unison, "You did that?"

Take an idea. Then turn it into a dream, chase the dream into something tangible, that is what I enjoy doing. However, once the dream is real and my mind is satisfied with the results, I lose interest and pursue another dream. I don't know why I'm that way. It's just my nature.

Once, I was at the Montana State Fair with my carpenter friend Scott. We were walking around, doing nothing in particular, just taking in the sights and the tight-fitting jeans of the ladies. America is the land of some grossly overweight people.

Scott said, "That one looks like two pigs stuffed in a gunnysack." I could visualize them instantly.

Then I saw a sign that said, "Your Handwriting Analyst Here by Televac."

"Good way to get a handwriting example of the general public without their full knowledge," I thought. It was quite an impressive looking machine.

"Go ahead, "I am curious what it will say." said Scott.

I wrote the name Joseph in my finest script on a slip of paper, following the machine's instructions inserted two dollars and the slip into the slot ... In less than thirty seconds, the results were in my hand. I read it to Scott:

"Your handwriting analysis by Televac. Your self-confidence is evidenced in your decisions. You never hesitate when the going gets rough. You have a shrewd mind and are imaginative. You usually lack initiative and need a push from your friends. You seem to be looking for something you will never find. You like to travel a good deal for all sorts of reasons. You enjoy helping others but will not give advice unless asked. You are convincingly good at the soft sell method. You appreciate beauty, especially the opposite sex. You are somewhat skeptical of new places and peoples."

"What a bunch of bullshit," Scott said.

I put the paper in my pocket and later pasted it in my journal.

Chapter twenty

"ZIHUATANEJO, MEXICO"

The withdrawal of my physical support from the restaurant was placing a tremendous amount of weight on Franca's shoulders. I knew it. I was concerned for her, but did my best to avoid being part. Soon she had a lawn man, a laundry girl, a dishwasher, a busgirl, an assistant cook, and waitress/hostess; still Franca was working too hard.

One night after the last of the help had left

I said to her "Let's sell this thing. It's becoming a monster. You are serving too many people. I am ready for a new adventure. I want my wife back. I now have a chef for a wife. What I want is a wife who is an ex-chef."

"I'm not ready to do that," she replied.

I have always respected Franca's decisions and knew that it would be wrong to press my will on her.

In 1996, I decided to go big game fishing, one of those spur of the moment things, decided that I wanted to catch a real big fish, one that was bigger than I was. So I walked down to the local travel agency and explained my desire.

Where do you want to go?" The clerk asked.

"I really don't care, just as long as I can catch a really big fish," I replied. Two weeks later Franca and I closed the restaurant for a week's vacation in Zihua-tanejo, Mexico. I fished several times, spent large sums of money on charters, and never got my fish. It never really mattered for I was hooked on Mexico, its people, its beauty, its unpredictability. We made two more vacation trips to the Pacific coast of Mexico. The last one was in a rented car with which we explored all the roads, nooks, and crannies along Mexico 200.

Franca discovered La Barra de Potosi and the beach of Playa Blanca. We found a nice little furnished beach house and rented it for a week of relaxation, sun, sea, and siestas. In the evening, we would walk the deserted coastline hand and hand watching the sun turn the skies into a glorious spectrum of colors. I fell in love with the place.

"Franca, I want to buy a small piece of land here, build a studio and a small house. This is the view I had been searching for" I said.

Franca's response to my idea was mild enthusiasm.

"I'm not going to give up the restaurant. But if you want to make Mexico your project that's fine with me, dearest husband." I smiled and kissed her neck.

On our flight, back to the United States all I could think about was Barra de Potosi. I had left a fishing rod and reel in the care of one of the local fishermen named Chilpa.

"If, when I go back down, Chilpa still has my fishing equipment, I'll start giving some serious considerations to the idea of building. If, on the other hand, he has lost or sold it, then I'll change my mind, for that will be an indication that the people of the village are not to be trusted."

Rested and ready, we reopened. Help was very difficult to find that season and what help there was, was difficult to work with. Once again, this forced Franca to stand in front of the huge Wolf range from opening to closing. I had little time to myself. I was beginning to feel my 60-odd years of life, I could think of nothing else but Mexico and fishing for Marlin, Sailfish, and Dorado

I have never felt comfortable in the presence of lots of people and the constant demands of the clientele that desired Franca's food were beginning to try my patience. I started thinking of diners as seagulls. I would work all afternoon setting the tables with fresh linens, flowers, silverware, and china. Franca would lovingly prepare roasts, fish, fowl, fresh bread, and desserts.

When all was ready, I would open the front door and visualize a flock of squawking, demanding seagulls that would crowd around the waiting tables; they would pick and choose, spill food, wine and enjoy themselves. When they had devoured as much as they could, they would all take flight, leaving a pile of money and the mess behind, for me the buss boy. I tried to disguise my feelings.

Franca can always see right through me. "You're doing me more harm than good," she said. The last customers had left and we were sitting at table nine, the one closest to the kitchen. My legs and feet hurt, dog tired, the restaurant in shambles.

"Let's sell," I asked.

"Let's stay open until the year 2000. I am not ready to do that yet, Joseph"

"I'm tired, dear," I replied. "And I'm starting to hate the restaurant."

"Why don't you go back to Mexico for a short while? I can run the restaurant by myself. I will find some decent help. Give me a month more and you can go." I kissed her hand and we finished our wine. Exhausted we went upstairs to sleep then meet the onslaught of the following day.

Now that Franca had given me her assurance that she would be able to handle her business without me. I began to make plans for a trip back to Mexico with the intention of buying a beachfront lot and building a new studio home for our retirement.

I knew what I wanted to do would require many tools and equipment for the Barra de Potosi was not a developed area. The road in and out was a badly rutted single lane dirt road. Electricity was there but service was unreliable at best. I started a shopping list, which was quite extensive and expensive. For starters, I needed a reliable truck, a generator, electric saws, drills, sanders, chainsaws, good grade exterior plywood, hand tools, more fishing equipment. I decided that I wanted to have my own fishing boat, needed an outboard motor, depth finder, lures, compass and anything else I could think of...

Every day I would scan the local papers looking at sale ads until I found the truck needed. It was a 1972 half-ton Chevy. After looking it over, I paid for it from some of my poker winnings, hired a mechanic to go completely over it, motor, brakes, shocks, electrical system, and then set to shopping.

The greatest thing about gambling money is that it's so very easy to spend. Just take a wad of cash, go to Costco, get a shopping cart, and start piling stuff into it. New skill saw, hydraulic jack, whatever. Never look at the price tag, just load the cart with all you need or want. A new pocketknife, why not? New out-board motor just put it in the back of the truck. By the time September arrived, the forest green truck was loaded and road-ready. I had managed to pack 1800 pounds of cargo into the back, even found a fourteen-foot long aluminum boat to put on top of the camper shell that covered the purchases.

I purchased cassette tapes in Spanish and English, and listened to them while driving to and from the poker games in Billings, Montana. A one hundred eighty mile round trip, first thing I would do before taking a seat at the card table was fill the gas tank just in case. The trip justified the expense as I won many thousands of dollars over the course of several years, and three Texas Hold Em tournaments. I never lost my cool or never became desperate.

I needed to learn a new language if I was going to succeed in my endeavors in Mexico. I had little driving experience in Mexico, but it was enough to have me well provisioned with water, tools, extra gasoline.

"The shortest route between two places is a straight line." With that axiom in mind, I unfolded the map of Mexico and the U.S., placed a ruler between the cities of Cody, Wyoming and Zihuatanejo, Mexico.

Reading the names of the cities and towns that fell closest to the ruler, I decided the route would be south to Eagle Pass and Piedras Negras with first a stop to see my good friend Tom Power in Utopia, Texas ... It seems like our lives have many parallels, Tom and I. In fact, he had decided to make that trip down with me. The plan was, I would drive to Utopia, pick him up, and we would make the trip to Zihuatanejo together. I said goodbye to my beautiful wife, set off for Texas and Mexico. When I pulled up to Tom's yard, he came out to greet me.

"I got bad news for you compadre," he said. "There's a hurricane. It just hit Acapulco. The highways are a mess, trees are down, and bridges are out. You ain't going to Mexico."

Disappointed I caught up on some much needed sleep. Next morning Tom drove me back to San Antonio in his Mercedes where I caught a one-way flight back to Cody, and reluctantly returned to helping Franca.

One night, I opened the door to greet the evening's first customers. After years of greeting people at the door, you develop a sense and can tell who will enjoy the place and who will not.

I said hello and then asked, "Do you have reservations?"

"No we do not," they answered. I could see from their frowning faces that I was not going to enjoy waiting on them and most assuredly, they were not going to enjoy my charming manners. I still had seating space. I invited them in, handed them a menu.

"This is tonight's main dinner listing along with the house specials of raviolis and tortellini. I will be with you in a minute"

"We were looking for spaghetti," the woman said.

"There's a Mexican restaurant on the corner, you might try there," I sent them away. That night I convinced Franca to close down the restaurant for ten days and make the trip to Zihuatanejo with me.

I started by saying, "You know dear, if you don't go you will miss an adventure of a life time" She was cool to the idea. "Think of all the haciendas and great restaurants we'll find." those were magical words. She relented.

At the end of October we closed the restaurant, got our pictures in the local paper. The caption: "Snowbird Flies South" was much better than the previous time." Man with Axe Silences Silver Dollar Bar."

To save a bit of money we decided to take a Greyhound bus back to my truck. After twenty-four hours of sitting in a bus and eating horrible food, we enjoyed a couple of days of great Texas hospitality and rest with Tom and his family.

Rested and enthusiastic, we climbed back into the pickup's cab and headed south at daybreak to Piedras Negras and the Mexican border. I estimated that we could make Saltillo before nightfall.

I knew it was most likely I would have to pay a large amount of import fees on the equipment I was carrying in the truck. Just the brand new outboard motor crated and stored beneath the plywood sheets was $7000; there was another $7000 in tools and deep sea fishing gear. I expected to pay around $1500 in import fees.

When we arrived at the customs- house, several armed guards directed us into the parking lot. My friend Tom had forewarned me that I would encounter bribery. I should offer only small amounts of money, $10, or $15dollars. I opened the truck door for Franca, hand-in-hand we walked over to the Mexican customs and immigration offices

I have learned in my travels that costume is a very important part of survival. For this adventure I had let my beard grow, wore and old fishing hat, placed a fishing rod in the rear window gun rack along with a couple of pot, pans, and a coffee pot. Customs, early in the morning was empty. We were the only foreigner's vehicle in the parking lot. Consequently, some six or seven pairs of Spanish eyes were eyeballing our truck.

"Bonita camioneta"I heard one say.

A neatly uniformed officer, who asked our business, met us at the entrance.

"I'm a fisherman; I and my wife are going to Zihuatanejo. I need an importation decal for my truck" as I shook his hand.

"Very nice truck," said the officer. "And the boat on top is it new?"

"No, Señor, I've had it for a long time."

"And the truck, have you had it a long time?"

"Oh yes. I bought it when I was a young man. I've had it for almost twenty years," I continued, "love it more than my own wife; I will be keeping this truck forever." They gave us forms to fill out. Did I have anything to declare? No, I had only camping and fishing equipment. How long were we going to stay? "Six months," I answered.

"But I can only issue you a permit for 30 days Señor."

I smiled broadly at him, "Señor, I want to do a lot of fishing and camping. I want to enjoy Mexico and its customs."

"Perhaps I could do you a favor?" the officer replied. I understood instantly and dug into a nearly empty wallet. I carried major credit cards and cash in my right boot. At that time, had $4000 stashed there.

"I understand. Thank you very much," handed him a $10 bill.

He took it, saying in perfect English. "So very little money for such big favors sir."

I could see his disappointment at the amount.

I explained that I was an artist and made very little money and that $10 was *mucho para mi*. He stood undecided; I could sympathize with him. Wages are low in Mexico.

"You must have a wife and children to take care of and I'm sure you have a big family." I continued to smile shaking his hand while slipping him a twenty-dollar bill. He returned my smile, went into the closed office, spoke with his compadre who got up from the desk and came over to the teller's window. He took my application forms and sent one of the guards out to check the serial numbers and registration numbers of my old Pickup. After verification, we received our permit stickers for the windshield. Back in the truck Franca asked what the exchange of money was about …

I let out a long sigh and said, "You don't want to know dear." Like the wonderful wife she is, her only reply was, "Oh."

The young man I bought the truck from had installed a pair of very loud exhaust mufflers. I had considered changing them to quieter ones but after driving the truck for a while, decided to keep them. Consequently, the 350 Horsepower engine would come to life with a roar, when I turned the key.

Backing carefully out and onto the highway, we pulled up to the gatehouse where I showed the guard the documents. He waved me through and into customs and inspection, where a sluggishly fat corporal greeted us.

I handed him the documents, which he briefly looked at, then he asked me.

"What do you have in the back?"

"Camping and fishing stuff," I replied.

"Please get out," he demanded "I must look in the back sir.

I took Franca's hand and said, "Didn't I tell you this was going to be an exciting trip. Stay there and don't get out unless I say its ok."

I got out. "Open up the back sir."

I complied, undoing the cables that were holding the aluminum skiff on to the top of the camper shell. Then, I opened up the back and lowered the tailgate. I had crated the outboard motor, expensive fishing rods, reels, and lures and hid it next to the cab under sheets of ¾-inch marine plywood. Then I put mattresses, blankets, clothes, and boxes on top of it and a small-scale model of the house I was planning to build. . The model had a removable roof, we had stuffed the interior with puzzles, teddy bears, and an assortment of small toys picked up at garage sales in Cody. They were presents for many of the children of the village of Potosi. I even stashed a half-gallon of Jack Daniels whiskey there for some of my newfound friends. Just inside the tailgate, I stored cooler, food, extra gasoline, and an old chainsaw Tom had given me. The first thing the custom man saw was the model house with its toys.

"What is that?"

"That's a present for the *niñas de mi compadre*." I answered politely.

"What are you doing with the wood?"

"There's an old man who lives on the beach, "He has no house. So I am bringing these to him so that he may have a house."

"What's under these pieces of wood?" he asked suspiciously, peering under the neatly stacked pile of plywood?

"Fishing things, "I am a fisherman," I replied as calmly as I could.

"You must take everything out," he said.

"Sir," I continued, "I cannot do that as I have a very bad heart, but if you wish to remove everything and put it back then I have no objections." The guard looked at the back of the truck. I could almost hear his mind grinding as he considered removing those sheets of plywood.

"Is the wood new?" he asked.

"No sir, it has nails in it."

"Perhaps we could come to an arrangement," the guard continued.

"Of course we can, I understand your position sir." I smiled broadly at him.

I returned to the truck, took my newly acquired documents, folded a $10 bill in with them, and returned to the waiting guard.

"I'm sure the papers are in order," I said as I handed them over to him. Taking the papers and the money, he looked them over, handed back the papers less cash and said, "Enjoy Mexico and have a safe trip."

"Thank you very much" I shook his hand, tied the boat back down, got into the cab.

Franca asked if everything was all right. "Yes, dear, we are on our way, didn't I tell you this was going to be a very interesting trip." Well I am not sure about that, I've never heard you tell so many lies." "Only when in Mexico and at the poker table, my dear."

"I think I should pee before we go."

"I wish you would wait a little bit longer." I said as I drove out of customs. Five miles down the road, I realized there would be no luxury rest rooms, I pulled over to the roadside, killed the engine, then waited for the dust to settle, traffic was light. I said to Franca, "Here you are dear." She looked at the roadside trash, the thorny scrub brush and cactus, gave me a puzzled look, and then said, "I have to go here?

"This is part of Mexico; I told you it would be an exciting trip." She said something under her breath that I did not catch as she got out of the truck.

I was beginning to love Mexico. We made Saltillo by dusk and found by trial and error a quaint hacienda located close to the heart of the city. It was a beautiful place with many ancient trees, flowers, and fountains. It reminded me of the Italian courtyards. The owners were very hospitable; the room was comfortable in size. After settling in for the night, we went to the dining room where we ate excellent grilled chicken. That along with a couple of glasses of wine made a great end of the first day of our Mexican adventure.

Early next morning after breakfast of fresh mango, papaya, melon, toast, and coffee, we paid the bill, $40 US including tips. I was really beginning to take pleasure in Mexico.

Our next destination for that day was San Luis de Potosi. We made the trip without incident and settled into an excellent hotel, found a great restaurant, after dinner we walked around admiring the beautiful architecture of that colonial city.

The morning sun found us on the road to Morelia. The map showed two roads that would bring us to our next destination, Limon. One road diverted to the east about fifty miles, the other one appeared to be relatively a straight shot, but was marked as a secondary road. I had already made up my mind to take the longer route. That is, until we reached the junction of the two.

Noon found us at that point. I pulled the truck off the road, got out to stretch my tired back, and look at the alternative route. The asphalt appeared to be in excellent condition. I decided to give it a go. Fifty miles less of driving was very tempting. After a roadside lunch in the high mountain country under the stand of beautiful old growth pines, we continued onward by the secondary road. It was great, mile after mile rolled by; at twenty miles, the road began to wind down into the jungle, the inclines were steep and I had to gear down, using the engine for braking. The dual mufflers rumbling like distant thunder, down and down we went. Thirty miles in, found us in the middle of a maze of cars, horses, mules, and throngs of people all jamming the road at the entrance of a cemetery. We were traveling on the Day of the Dead.

I should have made a u-turn and retreated, but my obstinate streak caused me to continue. Slowly, very slowly, I eased our way through the crowd of celebrators. It took the better part of 30 minutes to clear the way.

Then we continued onward another mile or so until we crossed a wide river. I wondered what sort of fish were swimming in its dark currents under the concrete bridge as the truck rumbled across it.

We paralleled the river for a while and soon came to an assortment of small unkempt adobe and stick shanties that made up the town of about fifty inhabitants. Chickens, dogs, children, pigs, and goats were wandering peacefully about, every one staring at us as we passed through.

Outside of the town, the pavement ended, replaced with small river rock. We were forty miles in on the secondary road. About halfway to the town of Limon, we saw a man with a donkey tied on a blue string and a big machete in his other hand. I stopped to ask, "*Esto Camino van a Limon?*" He looked up at the skiff tied on top of the truck, then curiously at us and then bobbed his head up and down.

"Si, si," he said pointing southward with his machete. Then he rattled on for a while longer, me not understanding a word.

He was probably saying something like, "You dumb gringo. Don't you know this road is the highway to many tombstones? You go, you don't come back."

I smiled and nodded my head in agreement. Then to make sure I understood, pointed at the now narrowing trail, and said, "Limon, si, si."

"Ok, we're on our way," I said to Franca.

I put the truck back in second and let out the clutch. We had not gone far when I had to scrape the hillside to let an oncoming bus come through. It was loaded with people, covered with dust, mud, and had "Limon Morelia" printed on a piece of cardboard taped to its cracked front window.

Feeling confident, I said to Franca, "If a bus can get through, the road can't be that bad."

We relaxed and started enjoying the ride through the jungle. It was not long before the road leveled out and the driving was less stressful.

We stopped on a downgrade and had some snacks and another cup of espresso, made over the flame of a Burns-O-Matic torch. It is the only way to travel. Franca gets out the camera and we take a few pictures of the huge trees draped with vines. I check the tires and notice that the left rear is a little low. Nothing to concern myself over, I decide. After all, we are almost to Limon. Rested and re-energized we go forward. There are huge tarantula spiders all over the place. We joke about spider crossings and then suddenly the road narrows to the point where the brush is scraping both sides of the cab. One side becomes a sheer drop off.

I do not want to alarm Franca so I say nothing, but I am very concerned. She is chatting away while I am watching the rear tire in the mirror.

It is definitely losing air. We come around a blind curve. The road hugs the mountainside, and then it starts down to a muddy river. There is no bridge, just a set of tracks leading into the water and exiting onto the opposite bank 75 feet away. The grade is steep both ways. I stop dumbfounded.

We are past the point of no return. I cannot turn around if I wanted to. The road is just too narrow. I get out and look at the river. It is running a brown muddy color but not too swiftly. I can see the tracks of the bus on the other side. I have no idea if the river is full of crocs, piranhas, leeches, or snakes and I am not going to find out by wading in.

If the bus made it, surely we can. I put the truck in low gear, look once more at the deflating tire, told Franca everything is fine, then with heart in my throat drive into the water. At midstream, it's seeping in under the doors, then finally the level ascends and we are on dry ground once again.

"See, I told you this was going to be an exciting trip."

To which Franca replied, "I don't know about that, but I need to pee, soon."

"Me too dear," I answer.

Shortly after that, we came upon a construction site, with men and machinery crushing rock for roadbed material. We pull in and find workers. Pointed at the almost flat tire and asked if he had a compressor. No such luck. However, he helps me to dig out the spare and change the tire. Happily, I give him ten dollars.

The remaining road is rocky but wide and under construction. Darkness finds us in Limon. It had taken hours to cover seventy or eighty miles, but we are still safe. Limon is a nasty town, drunks everywhere. Who can blame them? People are walking around in costumes. It looks like a scene from The Night of the Living Dead. We found a sleazy motel with high concrete walls topped with jagged glass enclosing the entire place and rented a room.

My wife's usual procedure when selecting a hotel is to consult travel guides, make personal inspections, and never stay in the first room offered. When she saw the accommodations, I simply said, "Not this time dear. We stay here." She did not protest. Dinner was not gourmet either. Some overcooked chicken and warm beer. We do not recommend Limon as a travel destination. The morning of our last day of travel, we refueled the truck and headed south. We have still to cross the Sierra Madre del Sur to reach the Pacific Coast and our destination of Barra de Potosi, just a few kilometers south of Zihuatanejo.

We were on pavement again and even though the highway is not in the best of repair, we laughed and joked about how it was a super-highway compared to the previous day's journey. We begin are assent into the heart of the rugged Sierra Madre del Sur mountains. A notation on the map says, the "*Espinoza del diabla*" The witch's spine.

Traffic was non-existent, the further we rode, the more the condition of the road deteriorated, with washed out sections, mudslides, boulders strewn all over the road. I felt like I was maneuvering through an obstacle course. Mile after mile, we followed the twisting, tortured, fragmented asphalt. My neck and shoulders ached from driving and shifting gears. I couldn't believe it, but it was actually worse than the previous day. It was uphill all the way. The truck was not at a loss for power but those 200 horses under the hood needed much fuel. I watched the gas gauge steadily lower.

Shortly before we reached the summit, we stopped for lunch and admired the magnificent vistas of the mountains. Concerned about our fuel supplies I undid the cables holding the aluminum skiff to the top of the camper, dug out five gallons of gas I had in reserve and poured them into the gas tank, then re-secured the load.

We then continued, onward and upward. At the summit, the roadway leveled out and its condition improved. About this time, a convoy of heavily armed soldiers passed us going in the opposite direction, six Humvees loaded with machine guns and men wearing helmets, bulletproof jackets, sunglasses, and helmets, all dressed ominously in black.

These were the first vehicles we encountered in over four hours of driving. As they passed, I had an uneasy feeling that not all was well.

Not five miles later, we are starting our descent. Suddenly, blocking the road were several large stones on top of which have been placed pieces of steel rebar. I came to a stop and said in amazement to Franca, "What the hell? Don't tell me this road is closed."

We sat there for a few seconds with the engine idling. Suddenly out of the roadside underbrush, two men wearing flower sacks over their heads with holes cut for their eyes appeared, waving pistols and shouting, "*Manos Arriba!*" The sacks and the guns were my immediate clue that not all was right with the situation.

I saw no sign of high power rifles and could tell in an instant that the pistols were cheap 22 caliber Saturday night specials. I made a quick decision.

"Get down!" I said to Franca. I shoved the truck into gear, pushed the gas pedal to the floor, let out the clutch. The truck leaped forward, rear tires squealing and smoking. I tried my best to avoid hitting the oil pan and the vital parts of the motor on the rocks as we crashed through the barrier.

Franca, whose vision was obstructed by my body, really did not know what was going on. I heard the first bullet hit the truck inches behind my head.

Ping! Followed by several more shots in rapid succession, Ping! Ping! Ping!

"Get down!" I yell at her.

"What?" She replies.

"Get down! The son's of bitches are shooting at us!"

Now we were through the barricade and picking up speed. Several more shots rung out, ping, ping, ping, and we were out of range.

"What is happening? Franca is asking me excitedly.

I was too busy watching the road, oil pressure, gas gauge, water gauge, shifting gears, checking the rear view mirror, trying to see if we are being pursued, to answer her.

Everything looked good, no smoke or noise coming from the motor, no one giving chase. I checked the brakes; they worked. After a few miles of speeding dangerously down the mountainside, I said to Franca, "I want to stop and check for damage."

Franca replied, "You do not stop until we get into Zihuatanejo. I do not care if I pee my pants."

"I told you this was going to be an exciting adventure."

With that, we broke into excited nervous laughter. That is how life is. One day you are enjoying yourself making plans and within seconds, you are likely to be dead.

We made it to Zihuatanejo late without other problems, found a nice hotel, and spent the night. In the morning, we examined the truck. There were two bullet holes directly in line with my head behind the cab. We found three more stitched into the back of the camper, one of which had made a direct hit on the half-gallon bottle of Jack Daniels that was in the back. The liquid soaked the Pentax and various lenses I had carefully packed away.

I knew immediately that that truck was never going back to the United States. Franca called our bank and cancelled the credit card that I had used for entry into Mexico, and never bothered to report the incident to the police.

To say that Franca was not too keen about Mexico is an understatement but she allowed me to have my way without ultimatums. Thus ended our Mexican adventure.

For the last engraving work, I specifically chose, at the factory in Cody, a pair of consecutively serial numbered Ballard Winchester rifles. I applied all my knowledge to those two rifles and executed with the greatest of skill every technique I had learned: Gold inlay, arabesque scroll, banknote style engraving, sculpted steel relief, layout, and lettering. I also took time to explain all the various tools and their purposes for the video. A proud ending to an engraving career that had a very shaky beginning.

September 1, 2001 was the last day Franca's Italian Dining was open. I had informed the Buffalo Bill Historical Center and the Cody Firearms Museum that Joseph, was retiring. The museum Director arranged that I would engrave these last rifles in the museum before the public, and videotape the process, for their permanent collection that included all my tools, books, notes, prints, negatives, molds, and models.

Amongst the items given to the museum is the little black book of poetry that the missionary from Calcutta had given me. I am ignorant of his name and cannot give the stranger I met while traveling to Italy, proper credit for his gift, his encouragement, and kindness

From my journal:

Dear Universal Mind,

I have not written you in a long time. I really don't have much to say except that life is going well and I'm happy. Thank you so much for entering my life. I know I am flawed and not deserving but I appreciate your consideration.

The closing note from my journal, written to me by my soul mate:

Joseph dear,

I like you because I love you. Although I love you because you are a child of God and an inheritor of the kingdom of heaven, and deep down you are full of the power, glory, and majesty that are uniquely yours.

Love, Franca

November, 2006, Barra de Potosí, Mexico

Dear, Universal Mind,

Thank you for giving me this day. Thank you for giving me my life. Thank you for giving me my beautiful wife. Thank you for such a great dog as Ace. Thank you for your blessings, which are many. Friday, I am filling "Lillian" with 250 liters of gasoline—then heading out onto the royal blue Pacific water in search of a fish larger than I am.

I know I have not been the best disciple—and in the scheme of things, I am but a dot. Here is the book I have promised, along with my sincerest thought:

I love you.

Your creation, Joseph

THE END

My 365 lb. blue marlin, Zihuatanejo Mexico 2005

Author's Notes

First, I must apologize to the reader for my lack of literary skills and for the fact that I have changed names for personal reasons, and for my lackadaisical record keeping. In many instances I have neglected to record the serial numbers of the weapons I have engraved, in others, I took no photos. Nor did I sign all of the rifles pistols or shotguns I have embellished. My way of marking the work depended on my mood. On most commission work, I would cut a small "j" in script and the year I completed the work, in some obscure place on the tag or grip. I have completed most of my favorite signed pieces during my years living in Cody Wyoming. Those I signed, Joseph, Cody WY.

I rarely enjoyed engraving pistols or revolvers, although I cut my share, the steel being tough and the hardness unpredictable. The weapons I dearly enjoyed were the lever action Winchesters and it was upon them that I lavished my skills. Every moment I spent at the vise was done with only one thought in mind. That thought was how to push myself to the next plateau of engraving skill. I have copied many of L.D.Nimschke and G. Young's engravings but the engravers I was to follow most closely were John and Conrad Ulrich. It started when I purchased a copy of R.L.Wilson's "THE WINCHESTER BOOK OF ENGRAVING."

The author's comments about the rarity and extraordinary engraving of one assemblage of history making weapons, was that they were beyond the reach of ordinary men. As I studied the photo, I came to the realization that I was a man gifted with all the skills necessary, to replicate closely every rifle in that photograph. The time and money were available to me, I set to work immediately on this project, and had it completed in three years. During that time, I realized that there was a very good market for excellent reproductions of the Ulrich's brother's works, especially for the models 1890, 1892, and 1894. I engraved several of each model on speculation and on demand of clients. The Winchester model 1876 rifle with its large flat frame of mildly heat-treated steel was an irresistible attraction for me. I engraved a total of six of them of which I was particularly proud, not only for the fact that they were my own designs, but the fact that I had developed my discipline to the point of being able to concentrate so intently for such an extended period of time.

The more challenging the engraving project was, the better I liked it. There was no greater satisfaction to me than to begin a project with the thought in my mind "I wonder if I can pull this off." This was particularly true of the Tiffany inspired model 94 Winchesters.

I was not confident that I would be able to copy it as the design and style of workmanship was unique to me. I purchased a model 1894 take down rifle in good mechanical condition with stocks of rather plain walnut and used it to do my experimenting on. It turned out to be a decent piece of work, but did not meet my standards; therefore, I sold it at a very reasonable price. I purchased another model 94 rifle, and applied what I had learned to it. The results are one of the most ornate model 94 rifles in existence. As a rule, I did my own stock fitting, finishing and carving using the highest grades of stock woods available to me. I also did my own metal polishing, for I was very particular about all aspects of my restorations, with the exception of the rifles bore that was of little importance as far as I was concerned.

My most favorite weapon to engrave was the model 1873 Winchester. Its shape lent it self so perfectly for engraving and never did any other rifle excite my imagination as did it. The steel frame was perfect in hardness and cut like butter, the flatness of the side plates and their shapes complemented my engravings; I did my most demanding bank note work on those frames.

The one I consider the most complex, I engraved with the theme of the Continental Railroad on both side plates and frame. I had discovered a print in and old book about the civil war. It had a scene of eighteen Negroes with tools over their shoulders, hands waving about leisurely, while a white overseer sat astride his horse, gloved hand raised in command. I could not resist the challenge.

Could I translate that complex drawing down to a space of four and one half square inches? I began the work by doing a carefully detailed tracing on Mylar plastic, then reducing it to the size of the side plate. I prepared the plate for drawing and transferred the reduction to the side-plate, drawing in the spaces between the figures rather than trying to draw each individual worker. Once I had the correct spaces then I started the engraving.

It was so intricate that I was sure I would become confused while working under the magnification of a twelve-power loupe. I decided to draw directly from the original print, all those faces, hands, feet, shoes, clothes, hoes, rakes, picks, shovels, and expressions rendered in steel. I had already started the cutting when I came to the realization that it was actually easier for me if I worked from the original print turned upside down. As the scene progressed, the details of the figures became so precise that I was making the cuts between heartbeats.

One day as I was working intently, Franca came to my studio door. "Excuse me for disturbing you," she said, "but I have an emergency in the restaurant." I looked up from my master piece and asked what the problem was." Her answer was," I need you to peel potatoes."

I never had a clock in my studio, nor did I listen to the radio while working. I wanted nothing to break my concentration, nor did I keep track of the hours I stood at my vise. I would mark the day I started a project on a calendar, work until I was exhausted then go fishing with Franca or go play poker for relaxation, taking as long a break as I needed, then return to the work. When the piece was completed, I would mark the calendar again, total up the days, multiply times two hundred, and determine the price of my labor. There is only one rifle that I could not find the mental stamina to finish as planned. That rifle was an 1866 Winchester that I decided to engrave as tributes to both C.M Russell and Fredrick Remington. I had intended to do all the engraving work in sculpted relief, however as the work progressed and was nearing its end I found the work so tiring that that in order to finish I completed the last vignette in bank note style, thus saving me another twenty hours of mind numbing labor. When it was completed, I had a mold made of the frame and the engraving then cast one in bronze for sale. It sold quickly, I exhibited the rifle and it sold the first day, it also brought the most money I ever received for my labors. Over the years, I sold many bronze casts of that rifle receiver.

Sculpting was more of a hobby than a passion, and I found it a good way to relieve the tensions that staring into a loupe hours at a time, brought on. Over the years, I modeled in clay a variety of animals and humans, made bronze castings of them and sold them. Some sold very well and others did not. A quarter of a century of industrious creativity produced a large volume of art. I have included in this book a few photos of my favorite works. The photos of those labors are on file in the archives of the McCracken Library located within the Buffalo Bill Historical Center. I again apologize to the reader for the lack of photographic sharpness in some instances.

978-0-595-45156-2
0-595-45156-X